788·36

D1577158

FILE COPY

FILE COPY

THE RECORDER AND ITS MUSIC

THE
RECORDER
AND
ITS MUSIC

Edgar Hunt

EULENBURG BOOKS
LONDON

Ernst Eulenburg Ltd
48 Great Marlborough Street
London W1V 2BN

First published by Herbert Jenkins in 1962

© Edgar Hunt, 1962, 1976. All rights reserved

This revised and enlarged edition first published in 1977
by Ernst Eulenburg Ltd

ISBN 0 903873 05 2 paperback
ISBN 0 903873 31 1 hardback

Printed and bound in England by
Caligraving Ltd, Thetford, Norfolk

Condition of sale. This book is sold subject to the condition that
it shall not, by way of trade or otherwise, be lent, re-sold, hired
out or otherwise circulated without the Publisher's prior consent,
in any form of binding or cover other than that in which it is published and without a similar condition including this condition
being imposed on the subsequent purchaser.

CONTENTS

FOREWORD
BY
DR CARL DOLMETSCH

The present-day meteoric return to popularity of the recorder — whose seductive tone charmed the ears of Henry VIII, Shakespeare and Pepys — is a development unparalleled in the history of any other musical instrument. When Arnold Dolmetsch produced his first recorders in 1919, he would no doubt have greeted with incredulity the information that the instrument was destined to become the most widely played of all serious instruments, ancient or modern. The manufacture, export and distribution of recorders has become one of the major musical instrument industries of the day. They are produced by the hundred thousand yearly and find their way to every corner of the globe. Furthermore, the publishing and selling of recorder music is a branch of the trade few music publishers or retailers can afford to ignore.

The recorder's many practical virtues — its relatively low cost, portability and hardiness — readily recommend it to music-lovers of every age and in all walks of life. On the one hand, the instrument satisfies the amateur seeking to play simple folk tunes and the like; on the other, it offers a challenge to the virtuoso player who aspires to play recorder music by Bach, Handel, Purcell, Telemann and their contemporaries.

The total eclipse of the recorder during the nineteenth century was happily to be no more than a temporary phase; thanks to the combined efforts of musicologists, scholars, teachers and other enthusiasts, its restoration to favour is assured. No-one could be better equipped to assess the recorder's place in the fields of music and education than Mr Edgar Hunt. His book is timely. To his survey of the instrument's history past and present, its literature and bibliography, the author has called on a vast store of knowledge acquired over many years of practical experience and research.

The recorder is often, however, a much misunderstood and maligned instrument. There are still too many critics among us who judge it by the limited technique of mediocre players. Before dismissing the recorder as a primitive instrument useful only as a step towards something better, they should know a little of its long and honourable history and the affection in which it was held by great composers of the past. The wheel has now turned full circle and modern writers are providing the recorder with a twentieth-century repertoire often demanding a degree of virtuosity comparable with that required to master any other solo instrument.

FOREWORD TO THE DUTCH EDITION

Unless a severe epidemic of myxomatosis succeeds in silencing us, the position of the recorder is an ineradicable one. The number of regular players throughout the whole world can be estimated at about half a million. Gratifying — and sometimes a little frightening — is the fact that Holland, through an abundance of home music-making, lower and higher education, vocational training, etc, contributes in a large proportion to this figure, as evidenced by the fact that approximately 50,000 recorders are bought here every year.

In Edgar Hunt's book we read how the development from an aristocratic and exclusive to a popular and everyday musical instrument has come about. No one can rival his great knowledge concerning the seventeenth- and eighteenth-century heyday of both instrument and literature. The fact that the reader will profit enormously from Edgar Hunt's knowledge through this Dutch translation seems to 'speak for itself' as much as the recorder does.

In all Dutch colleges of music the recorder is now taught as a principal study — a situation to which Kees Otten, in collaboration with Joannes Collette, gave the intial impetus in 1949. As a result, final examinations now ask detailed questions about the construction, history and literature of the instrument, and I therefore wholeheartedly recommend this excellent book to serious students too.

Amsterdam, 1966   Frans Brüggen

PREFACE
TO THE FIRST EDITION

In writing this book about the recorder, I have attempted to trace its history and position in the world of music, to provide the background to the employment of the instrument in the performance of its own music. In order to concentrate on this, the scope of the book has been limited deliberately, and the temptation to include lists of such items as gramophone records or of music for school use has been resisted. Such lists would soon be out of date, and, in any case, the information can be as easily obtained from the manufacturers or publishers themselves. Rather it is hoped that teachers may be encouraged to explore more of the recorder's own repertory after reading these pages.

When I was first invited to write this book, I thought, since so much of my life has been, and is, devoted to teaching the recorder, editing music for it, and in designing some of the instruments, how easy it would be! But, faced with a blank sheet of paper in my typewriter, I realized how much had to be done before a word could be written. If such a book was to have any value, I had to go over my first researches again in the light of later experience, re-reading and revising notes made in the 30s when, to most musicians, the recorder was unknown or obsolete.

The great difference between the 30s and now is the growth of interest in musical instruments in general, not only amongst musicians, but amongst the reading public; as witness the large number of books devoted to them, and the development of scholarship in this field.

One of these books on musical instruments (Pelican, edited by Anthony Baines) has little to say on the recorder, but offers this wise comment (p. 230):

> '. . . The prominence given to the little descant size today brings a false impression of recorder-playing of the past, both of the consort period and of Bach's day, when the treble was all-important . . .'

To correct this impression and to give a better perspective is one of my chief aims in this book.

Most of the recorders in this country belong to the baroque period, and our modern instruments are modelled on them. So, in order to study the earlier renaissance recorders, visits to some of the great collections of the continent were undertaken during 1960: first of all to Nürnberg and Munich, then to Brussels, Linz and Vienna, and finally to Paris, Antwerp and The Hague. It is pleasant to record my gratitude here to their curators for all their help, and in particualr to Dr Leonie von Wilckens of the German National Museum at Nürnberg, to Dr H. R. Weihrauch and his assistants of the Bavarian National Museum at Munich, to Monsieur Demeyer of the Royal Conservatoire of Music at Brussels, to the curator at Linz-Donau, to Dr Victor Luithlen of the Kunsthistorisches Museum at Vienna, to Monsieur Georges Migot of the National Conservatoire of Music at Paris, to Madame Thibault de Chambure of Paris and to the schoolmaster at La Couture-Boussey, to Dr Jeannine Douillez of the Vleeshuis at Antwerp, and, last but not least, to Dr J. H. van der Meer of the Gemeentemuseum at The Hague.

Those were the curators of the museums and collections which I was able to visit. There were many others who kindly furnished me with lists and other information relating to recorders in their keeping. These include Dr Wolfgang Schneewind of the Historical Museum at Basle, Dr Alfred Berner of the Institute for Musicology at Berlin, Dr Rubhardt of the Karl Marx University at Leipzig, Constantin Alexandrovitch Wertkow of the Institute of Theatre, Music and Cinematography at Leningrad, Dr Alens Plessingerová of the Národní Museum at Prague, Dr Ernst Emsheimer of the Musikhistoriska Museet at Stockholm, and Dr William Lichtenwanger of the Library of Congress, Washington, and his assistant Miss Gilliam. All have been most helpful.

In England the museums at Chester, Manchester, Bury St Edmunds and in London the Horniman, Victoria and Albert, and Donaldson museums have been visited; nor must Messrs Glen of Scotland's Royal Mile be forgotten. Mrs Jenkins of the Horniman Museum also furnished me with information about some collections behind the Iron Curtain.

Then there were my friends, Kurt Pitsch of Linz-Donau who enabled me to see so much in a brief visit to Linz and Vienna, Jean Henry who helped me in a similar way when I visited Paris, Kurt Ziener of Copenhagen who provided information regarding the recorder in Denmark and the instruments in the Clodius Collection, and Emil Brauer of Krönberg—a friend of forty years' standing—who recalled for me the early days of the revival in Germany. To all I am most grateful.

It is one of an author's most pleasant duties to thank all those who have helped his work, and there are many more in different parts of the world to whom such thanks are due, including the Secretaries of the Overseas Centres of Trinity College of Music and many others who have supplied information about the recorder in their districts—sometimes a long and interesting letter, at others a 'nil return'.

Nearer home Dr Walter Bergmann has given much encouragement and generous help with translations from the old German of Agricola, Mattheson and others. Not only has he helped in these immediate ways; but in a much wider field, by promoting concerts of exceptional quality, providing opportunities to hear and perform in some of the finest masterpieces of music in which recorders take part—works such as Bach's Cantata 39, Purcell's Ode for St Cecilia's Day (1692), Jeremiah Clarke's Music on Purcell's Death and Telemann's Concerto Grosso for two recorders, two oboes and strings.

Others who have helped with translations and correspondence include Miss Erika Seelig (German), Mrs Natasha Lytton and Mr Hugh Richardson (Russian), and Mr Zoltan Lukács (Hungarian).

Dr Carl Dolmetsch, CBE, besides generously contributing the foreword to this book, has read the manuscript with great care. Most of his suggestions have been incorporated in the text, but there still remain some points on which we must agree to differ! For instance, the use of the word 'fipple'. Dr Dolmetsch uses it to describe the 'lip' of the recorder: I prefer to apply it, following Welch, to the block which part-closes the end of the tube to form the wind-way. In old English 'fipple' meant 'under lip'. Now, if you look at the 'bec' or beak of the flûte à bec or recorder, you will see that the under lip is formed by this block or fipple.

Every writer on the recorder must acknowledge his debt to Christopher Welch who provided so much accurately documented information in his famous 'Six Lectures'. Having accepted Welch's derivation of 'recorder' for many years (from 'to record' meaning 'to sing like a bird'), it came as something of a surprise to receive in 1954 a letter from an expert in linguistics, Mr G. W. Turner of Christchurch, New Zealand, suggesting that the instrument came long before the bird-song. Mr Turner has convinced me, and I am grateful to him for thus correcting Welch.

Messrs Schott & Co Ltd have allowed me to reproduce short extracts from their publications in Figs. 16, 22, 31, 32 and 33.

Of the many friends among members of the Galpin Society, Mr Eric Halfpenny has allowed me to reproduce his X-ray photograph of the heads of two of Bressan's recorders, while Mr Guy Oldham saved me many hours of measuring by placing at my disposal the vital statistics of the sixteenth-century recorders which he had measured in Brussels, Paris and Vienna. To them and to many other friends among the members of The Galpin Society, The Royal Musical Association, the Society of Recorder Players, and colleagues and students of Trinity College of Music I offer my warmest thanks for their interest and encouragement.

Chesham Bois, 1962   **EDGAR HUNT**

PREFACE
TO THE SECOND EDITION

The appearance of this book in paperback form has provided me with the opportunity to revise and rewrite much of the text—particularly the last three chapters—as so much has happened in the course of the last fourteen years. In 1962 I had not met Frans Brüggen whose playing and teaching have done so much to advance recorder technique and the position of the recorder in the world of musicians. In 1963 an American edition was published by W.W. Norton & Company, Inc. which allowed me to correct a few errors which had been noticed in the original, and these corrections were also incorporated in subsequent printings in England. In 1966 a Dutch translation appeared under the imprint of Zomer & Keuning of Wageningen to which Frans Brüggen contributed an introduction; but now after these twelve years the perspective is so different that a new edition is essential. At the same time a French translation is in production, by Editions Zurfluh of Paris, for which the revised text is being used.

Chesham Bois, 1976   **EDGAR HUNT**

*To Max Champion
who shared with me
the excitement of discovery,
and to the members of
The Society of Recorder Players*

AUTHOR'S NOTES

The 'continuo' is not an instrument, but describes a part which can be played on a harpsichord or spinet, with or without a bass viol or violoncello. It can also be played on a pianoforte or organ, or, with suitable modifications, on a harp, lute or guitar.

The diagrams in Chapter VI of the vibration patterns of the recorder are diagrams to show the positions of the nodes and antinodes, for comparison with the string diagrams. They do not pretend to be pictures of what it would look like if one blew smoke into a glass recorder!

The pitch of notes is shown in accordance with the following table:

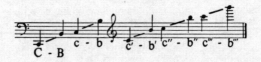

LIST OF PLATES

1

THE ORIGIN OF THE RECORDER

This book is about a family of musical wind instruments called 'recorders'. As the word 'recorder' can mean so many different things, from a legal official to a machine for recording sound, we must begin by defining what is meant by 'a recorder' in this book, and then try to explain its name.

A recorder is a tube, one end of which is partly blocked, and shaped to form a 'whistle' mouthpiece (Fig. 1). Here the tube is almost closed by a plug called the 'fipple', leaving a narrow channel or 'wind-way' through which the player's breath is directed, across an opening in one side of the tube, against the sharp edge of the 'lip', setting up vibrations. These vibrations are in turn communicated to the air in the tube. Holes in the side of the tube, governed by the player's fingers, modify the pitch of these vibrations to give a musical scale.

Fig. 1

Such a description could fit a number of instruments which can be classed as 'whistles' or 'fipple flutes'; so to arrive at our recorder we must go into greater detail. The chief difference which separates it from other fipple flutes—and this class of instruments includes flageolets, folk-dance pipes, penny whistles, and even the ocarina—is the fact that the recorder has a thumb hole in addition to seven finger holes. This feature is found on the earliest examples and was noticed by Shakespeare, when Hamlet described how to play a recorder: 'govern these ventages with your fingers and the thumb, give it breath with your mouth, and it will discourse most eloquent music, look you, these are the stops'. This thumb hole (together with the seven finger holes) separates the recorder from all the flageolets and various hybrid flutes that are its cousins, and is still its distinguishing characteristic.

Another feature of the recorder is its tapering bore. This has been subject to variation over the years, and its principle is shared with many other flutes; so it cannot be claimed as a distinguishing feature. However, it is generally cylindrical near the mouthpiece, getting smaller in the part with the finger holes, sometimes straightening out again towards the other end. This taper is the reverse of the taper of the oboes, bassoons and saxophones, which is smallest near the mouthpiece.

Although the recorder is frequently manufactured out of a plastic material, or made of ivory, wood is its natural material, and it is classed with the other flutes, oboes and clarinets as a 'woodwind' instrument. On the other hand, it is not regarded as an 'orchestral' instrument; for, although Purcell, Bach and Handel used recorders in some of their orchestral scores, the instrument missed the period of the orchestra's greatest development, the age of Haydn, Mozart and Beethoven, and so is not to be found in the modern symphony orchestra.

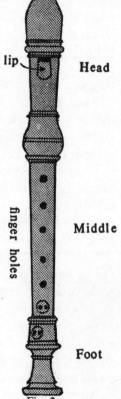

Fig. 2

The average recorder (Fig. 2) is made in three parts, known respectively as the head, which includes the mouthpiece, fipple or block and the lip; the middle joint with the six finger holes and thumb hole; and the foot joint with the seventh finger hole, which on the larger members of the family is covered with an open-standing key. In the case of some of the smaller recorders, the middle and foot joints are made as one, the lowest hole being drilled to one side.

Enough has now been written to give the reader some idea of what a recorder is; the picture will become clearer as more detail is added, and as descriptions are coupled with illustrations.

*   *   *

Next we come to the instrument's name— 'the recorder'. The generally accepted derivation is from the root verb 'to record' which has many meanings besides the basic one of 'to write down something in order that it can be remembered later'. One of these is 'to sing like a bird', and it at first seems obvious that the association is with the instrument's birdlike tone quality—an instrument that sings like a bird. In the eighteenth century the verb was used among bird fanciers to describe the first attempts of a bird to sing. The poets provide many examples of this use, such as:

> ... to the lute
> She sung and made the night-bird mute,
> That still records with moan.
>
> Shakespeare, *Pericles*
>
> They longed to see the day, to hear the lark
> Record her hymns and chant her carols blest.
>
> Fairfax, *Tasso*
>
> Now birds record new harmonie,
> And trees do whistle melodies;
> Now every thing that nature breeds
> Doth clad itself in pleasant weedes.
>
> Thomas Watson in *England's Helicon*

This use of the word is not necessarily confined to birds, but may be transferred to humans:

> ... By no means; no, boys;
> I am the man reserved for air, 'tis my part;
> And if she be not rock my voice shall reach her.
> Ye may record a little, or ye may whistle,
> As time shall minister: but for main singing,
> Pray ye satisfy yourselves: away, be careful.
>
> Beaumont and Fletcher, *Monsieur Thomas*

As Welch points out, it is unlikely that these serenaders were provided with recorders to play on; so here is another shade of meaning—'to hum softly'—and this finds a place in the dictionary also. Now, when one is humming softly, one is generally remembering a tune that one has heard before.

This surely brings us full circle to the Latin *Recordari*, the heart of which is COR, and which Dr Smith tells us means 'to think over, bethink oneself of, be mindful of; to call to mind, remember, recollect'. Writing in The Galpin Journal, (Vol.X, May 1957), Mr Brian Trowell draws attention to the Italian *Ricordo*, meaning 'remembrance, souvenir, keepsake, memento, sign of friendship, token, note'; and to a very interesting reference, in the household accounts of Henry Earl of Derby (later King Henry IV) for 1388, to payment for *i. fistula nomine Ricordo* (=a pipe called a 'memento')—possibly the first reference to our instrument.

The search for the first recorder is confused by the word 'flute' —sometimes it is used as a generic term, covering all sorts of wind instruments, at others referring to one kind in particular. Chaucer (c.1340–1400) does not mention our recorder, but he often does the flute. Was his 'gay young Squire' a recorder player—'singinge he was or floytinge al the day'? We shall never know; but remembering that one of the French names for the recorder was *la flûte douce*, there is the possibility that the 'doucet' might be the fourteenth-century name for the recorder, and that it was to this instrument that Chaucer referred in his *House of Fame:*

> That craftely begunne pype
> Bothe in doucet and rede.

Apart from **Henry's** *Ricordo* the earliest reference to our recorder may be in the romance, the *Squyr of Lowe Degre*, to which Welch assigns 1475, but Galpin c. 1400, as a probable date:

> There was myrth and melody
> With harp, getron and sautry,
> With rote, ribible and clokarde,
> With pypes, organs and bumbarde,
> With other mynstrelles them amonge,
> With sytolphe and with sautry songe,
> With fydle, recorde, and dowcemere,
> With trompette and with claryon clere,
> With dulcet pipes of many cordes.

If Galpin should be wrong in this instance, priority must be claimed for the *Promptorium Parvulorum,* the earliest English-Latin dictionary in existance, compiled by a Dominican friar of (King's) Lynn. There it is called a 'lytyl pype' and translated by *canula.* The date of the *Promptorium* is given as 1440, but Welch points out that a much earlier work, *Campus Florum,* is given as the authority for the translation, and the date of this latter work is probably c. 1359.

The recorder figures again in the catalogue of instruments in the

Scottish poem, the *Buke of the Howlate* (=Owl), *maid be* (=made by) *Holland*, c. 1450:

All thus our ladye they lofe, with liking and list,
　　Menstralis and musicians mo than I mene may,
The psaltery, the citholis, the soft cytharist,
　　The croude, and the monycordis, the gythornis gay,
The rote, and the recordour, the ribup, and rist,
　　The trump, and the taburn, the tympane but tray;
The lilt pype and the lute, the cithill in fist,
　　The dulsate, and the dulsacordis, the schalm of assay;
The amyable organis usit full oft,
　　Clarions loude knelis,
　　Portatvis and bellis,
　　Cymbaclanis in the cellis
　　That soundis so soft.

And in yet another of these catalogues, this time from a Cornish miracle play (again quoting Welch, with the translation by the editor of the play, a Mr Norris):

Rex DD	King David
wethong menstrels ha tabours	Blow minstrels and tabours;
trey-hans harpes ha trompours	Three hundred harps and trumpets;
cythol crowd fylh ha savtry	Dulcimer, fiddle, viol, and sawtry,
psalmus gyttrens ha nakrys	Shawms, lutes, and kettledrums;
organs in weth cymbalys	Organs, also cymbals,
recordys ha symphony.	Recorders, and symphony.

The fifteenth century is given as the probable date of this miracle play. There can be no doubt that these early poems refer to one particular instrument, whether it be spelt recorde, recordour or recordys, and we must note that the *Promptorium* also mentions the flute—so the two are distinct there.

These poems go to show the recorder was known, if not from Land's End to John O'Groats, at least from Cornwall to Scotland, and trace it back to the fifteenth century as an instrument, whereas it would appear that the birds did not record until the latter part of the sixteenth century. Is it not possible, therefore, that the instrument came first, and that the birds were said to record when they sounded like a particular kind of flute? If that is true, the following quotation, which may be remembered by some madrigal singers, refers directly to the recorder:

> Then tune to us, sweet bird, thy shrill recorder.
>
> Edward Johnson 'Come, blessed bird'
> from *The Triumphs of Oriana,* 1601

Another quotation disappointingly refers not to our instrument, but to a toy nightingale whistle:

> The nymph did earnestly contest
> whether the birds or she recorded best.
>
> Browne, *Britannia's Pastorals*

as the poet later explains that the nymph was only playing on:

> . . . a quill
> Wrought by the hand of Pan, which she did fill
> Half full with water; . . .

*   *   *

The recorder has had many different names in different languages, and deriving from the instrument's various features: its beak, the fipple or block, its sweetness of tone, the fact that it is held straight in front of the player, possible English origins, and to distinguish it from the German flute. Classified by languages they are:

English	*German*	*Italian*	*French*
Recorder			
Consort flute			flûte à neuf trous
	Schnabelflöte		flûte à bec
		Flauto dolce	flûte douce
Fipple flute	Blockflöte		
	Längsflöte	Flauto dritto	
English flute			flûte d'Angleterre
Common flute			
	Handflöte		

At certain times in its history the recorder has been known sim-

6

ply as 'the flute' *(flûte, Flöte, flauto)*; but at these times the transverse flute has been clearly distinguished by one of its names: *traversière, flauto traverso,* German flute, *Querflöte* or *Flûte d'Allemande.*

The various members of the recorder family have their different names, and here some confusion exists between the English and German systems of naming them. Our English nomenclature is based on the recognition of the treble (f´) recorder as the chief member of the family. Besides being the soloist of the family, it leads the three-part group; treble, mean (or tenor) and bass. The range of this group can then be extended downwards by the greatbass, and upwards by the descant and sopranino (Plate I). Thus all the recorders in C and F are given key positions in the scheme of things. Any exceptional sizes can be identified, either according to the eighteenth-century method, reckoning from the treble (such as 'sixth flute'), by allotting some special name (such as 'voice flute'), or by qualifying one of the main names (such as 'tenor in B flat'—instead of in C).

The German method is to use the voice names: Sopran, Alt, Tenor and Bass for the recorders in c″, f′, c′ and f. This method has been imported into the United States of America by musicians who settled there (from Germany) before World War II, and through the use of German music publications. The table at the top of page eight should help to clarify this matter. In it some of the early names, from the sixteenth to eighteenth centuries, have been included.

The fact that we cannot trace the name of our instrument back much before the fifteenth century need not prevent us from giving the recorder an earlier origin, possibly to the twelfth century. One thing is certain. The recorder was not suddenly invented, but was developed gradually from folk instruments of the whistle family. Most European folk whistles are narrow-bored instruments with six finger holes, depending on overblowing at the octave, and giving their best sounds as octave harmonics. If the maker were to keep the same length of pipe, but increased the diameter of the bore, the resulting instrument would have stronger fundamentals, but would yield the octaves less readily.

With six finger holes seven notes can be sounded as fundamentals, and these holes can be spaced to give a diatonic scale. They

Lowest note	English names	16th-cent. Virdung & Agricola	17th-cent. Praetorius	18th-cent. names	German names
g"			Klein Flottlein or Exilent		
f"	*Sopranino*		*Flautino alla vigesima seconda*	Octave flute or Flauto Piccolo	*Sopranino*
d"	Sixth flute		Discant	Sixth flute	
c"	*Descant*		Discant	Fifth flute	*Sopran*
b' flat				Fourth flute	
a'				Third flute	
g'	Treble in G	Discant	Alt		
f'	*Treble*			Flute or Concert flute	*Alt*
e' flat	Alto in E flat				
d'	*Alto* or Voice flute			Voice flute	
c'	*Tenor*	Tenor or Alt-tenor	Tenor	Tenor	*Tenor*
b flat	Tenor in B flat				
a					
g	Bass in G				(Tenor in A)
f	*Bass*	Bass	Bassett	Bass	Bass
c	Great Bass				Gross-bass
B flat			Bass		
F	(Double Bass)		Gross-bass		

can be tuned to the seven degrees of a major scale, and the top doh can be produced as an octave harmonic. If the bore is narrow a second octave and more of harmonics can be produced, and that is what happens in the penny whistle. If, on the other hand, the maker wishes to enhance the quality of the lowest octave and produce a mellow-toned instrument, he can enlarge the bore and sacrifice the higher notes. To compensate for this sacrifice, the range can be increased a little by adding to the number of finger holes within the limits of the player's two hands.

Folk instruments (Plate II) with a whistle mouthpiece are to be found in so many parts of the world that one cannot point to a particular one and say 'this is the father of the recorder'. These folk instruments do, however, provide the rough information and

*in the orchestra for Monteverdi's *Orfeo* (1607)

experimental material from which a craftsman might, given suitable tools, make a recorder.

What tools are necessary for making a recorder? Tools for boring and turning. The boring is probably the hardest part and a false move here could wreck the work. In the East bamboo provides a handy tube, but this is not indigenous to Europe; and the narrow bore of most European whistle flutes may be largely due to the prevalence of more slender pith-centred materials. In the case of early wooden recorders it is probable that the initial bore was burnt out and then enlarged to the desired shape. There can be little doubt but that the earliest extant recorders are craftsman-made art instruments which have left folk elements far behind.

The early recorders in the museums of Europe belong to the end of the fifteenth and beginning of the sixteenth centuries. So we must turn elsewhere, to paintings and sculpture, to know what earlier recorders looked like. Here we face a difficulty. Short of drawing a diagram, it is very difficult for any artist to show without doubt that he is drawing or carving a recorder and not some other wind instrument.

Some illustrations which used to be claimed, following Galpin, as showing recorders are now seen to be of other instruments. For instance, that in a Psalter in Glasgow University Library is some form of bagpipe, another in the Ormesby Psalter in the Bodleian Library is more probably a shawm, in view of its taper and the lack of the recorder's characteristic lip.

Carvings in England which may be supposed to represent recorders are listed by Galpin as follows:

13th Cent.   Chichester (carved choir stall)
15th Cent.   Boston, Manchester and Beverley (St Mary's)
16th Cent.   Cirencester (double recorder)

In addition, it is thought by some that the third figure from the right hand end of the statues in front of the Musician's Gallery in Exeter Cathedral is holding a recorder, though others think it is a shawm. The Cathedral was built between 1220 and 1370 and the gallery is high in the north wall of the nave. The carvings are very well preserved, being inside the building and out of reach; but even so the search for more exact information about the recorder of that time is not greatly helped. The carvings in Cirencester Church have been less fortunate. The double recorder, which is illustrated in some books, can no longer be distinguished. It was on one of the roof bosses and is now worn away by the action of the weather and the twentieth-century atmosphere. There is, however, at Exeter a beautiful fourteenth-century carving in wood, of the shepherds and angels at the Nativity, which shows a tenor recorder in the hands of one of the shepherds.

One thing these representations of the recorder have in common is their simple design. They look like the forerunners of the sixteenth-century recorders which have come down to us in the museums of Europe. And yet, because of the lack of detail in pictures to which we have referred, there remains an element of doubt whether we are looking at recorders or six-holed folk instruments. In a five-hundred page book of *Music in the Middle Ages* Gustave Reese allots only one paragraph to the flutes. In this he writes: '... The long flute—the *flûte douce* in France, recorder in England, *Blockflöte* in Germany—was a whistle-flute with a softer tone (than the flajolet or flageolet) and usually with six holes . . .' On what authority does Reese make this statement? In the chapter in question he is writing about music of the twelfth and thirteenth centuries, but nothing of significance is added in the following chapters to explain how the real recorder (with eight holes) suddenly appeared in time for the sixteenth century, when it proved to be pretty well standardized in Italy, France, Germany and England as an instrument with holes for seven fingers and a thumb.

Perhaps in looking at these pictures and carvings we are so anxious to find a recorder in them that we are prepared to find one in any straight piece of wood that appears to be blown by the man, woman or angel who holds it. Perhaps Reese is right and the twelfth and thirteenth centuries knew only six-holed *flûtes à bec,* and the true recorder appeared at the same time as its name at the beginning of the fifteenth-century. There is a recorder of this period in the Gemeentemuseum at The Hague. It is of elmwood about 11¾ inches long; and was discovered under a fifteenth-century house at Dordrecht. This instrument, a *flûte à neuf trous,* is in one piece, and appears to have had metal or ivory rings at the ends. It is possible that this is the earliest surviving recorder. (Plate III)

2

THE HISTORY OF THE RECORDER—PART I

Periods of artistic activity seldom exactly fit with the centuries by which we measure the passage of time, and their beginnings and ending vary in different countries. So, instead of giving this chapter a cumbersome title, such as 'The Recorder in the Renaissance and early Baroque', our first period will cover the time during which composers did not always specify exactly which instruments should play their instrumental and even vocal music; and when recorder

Fig. 3. From the *Fontegara* of Ganassi, Venice, 1535

players used the simpler wide-bored instruments. It will cover roughly the period up to, in England, the Restoration of the Monarchy in 1660. Such dates, however, may be misleading: recorder players did not suddenly give up their old recorders and buy new ones, nor did composers immediately change their habits of writing. But allowing for such overlaps of usage, that date at least provides a useful landmark in English music.

Leaving the doubts of the Middle Ages behind, our first period will start with the presumed date of the earliest extant recorders and such documentary evidence as may be coupled with them. The precise date might be as late as 1500; it is more probably nearer 1450; but could possibly be as early as 1400—in fact, not far separated from the word 'recorder' which has already been discussed. One thing, however, is certain, and that is: the early recorders were the ripe fruits of generations of craftsmen who understood what they were doing in the treatment of wood and other materials, and in the musical results of their labours. The experiments and mistakes had disappeared, and what remained was the work of true experts in a complex craft.

What a wonderful time for music the Renaissance must have been! We must remember that in the Middle Ages the Church had been dictator in matters of learning, and the Church favoured vocal music. Instrumental performers were generally classed with jugglers and other showmen, and were social outcasts. The sacraments of the Church were refused them and they were unprotected by Civil Law.

Yet these motley minstrels were necessary to society, to entertain and help the people to make the most of a festivity. Their popularity was vicarious. They tried to give themselves a kind of respectability by organizing themselves into guilds like the various groups of craftsmen. The *Confrèrie et Corporation des Ménestrels de Paris* was formed in 1321 under the leadership of *le Roi des Ménestrels,* but its members must have seemed as phoney to the craftsmen of those days as a member of a musicians' union might appear to a stevedore. In 1506 we read that the city of Basel forbade jugglers to wear trousers, and a Statute of 39 Eliz. declared that all fiddlers were rogues—except those of Chester. This special privilege was due to the fact that a crowd of minstrels had, many years before, been gathered at some festivity in Chester and while there had been able to frighten away an army of invading Welshmen! An exploit which was suitably rewarded.

With the growth of the merchant class and the growing power of the guilds, the city Waits were changing their roles from night watchmen to town band; and in the world of music a purely instrumental style, distinct from the calypso-like songs of the troubadours and from the music of the Church, was emerging. Secular vocal music was also advancing.

Some light on musical thought in the fifteenth century can be gained from a very interesting MS in the Royal Library at the British Museum (18. D. II); for on its vellum pages, after the genealogy of the Percys, are transcribed some 32 verses known as the Musical Proverbs of Leckingfield. These Musical Proverbs were written on the roof and walls of the garret of the New Lodge of Leckingfield Manor House. Of the Manor House not a stone remains. It seems to have been a fine place to judge by Leland's description (c. 1538), but by 1574 it was in sad disrepair, and was eventually pulled down. So we are grateful to the scribe William Peeris, who rescued these Proverbs from oblivion, and who described himself as 'clerke and preste to the right nobill Erle Henry the VII Erle of Narthumberlande'. The verses start off with 'putagoras and tuball', and after acknowledging a debt to the past, with a plea for simplicity, we come to some apt remarks about singing. Then each instrument has its verse: the harp, the clavichord, 'A slac strynge in a virginall soundithe not aright', 'Immoderate wyndes in a clarion causithe it for to rage' and so on, and in due course:

> The recorder of his kynde the meane dothe desyre
> Manyfolde fyngerynge & stoppes bryngithe hy from his tunes clere
> Who so lyst to handill an instrument so goode
> Must se in his many fyngerynge that he kepe tyme stop and moode.

In basic English this probably means: Of the recorder family the tenor (or meane) is the favourite: clear notes are produced from it by means of fingerings and cross-fingerings: he who would like to play well on such a good instrument, must see that in rapid passages he keeps time, and plays the right notes with the right fingering.

At this time the English throne was occupied by a succession of kings with an ear for music, as a glance at the records of the Privy Purse and of the Lord Chamberlain can prove. In the time of King Henry VII we read of 20 shillings paid 'to Arnolde pleyer at recorders' and in 1492 on February 14 'to the childe that playeth on the records, 20 shillings' and a little later 'To Gwillim for flotes with a case, 70 shillings'.

In the time of King Edward VI there are the names of five court flute players: John de Severnacke, Guillam Troche, Guillam Deventt, Piero Guye and Nicholas Pewell. In the reign of Queen Elizabeth we find:

> Pyro Guy flute
> Thomas Paginton flute
> Jacobo Fonyarde flute
> Nicholas Laneer vn de lez flutes

Did they play the recorder as well? By 1603 six members of the Venetian family of Bassano had arrived, and the list in connection with the funeral of Queen Elizabeth includes:

Recorders	Augustine Bassano	Jeromino Bassano
	Arthur Bassano	Alphonso Lanier
	Andrea Bassano	Robert Baker
	Edward Bassano	
Flutes	Piero Guy	Peter Edney
	Nicholas Lanier	Innocent Lanier
	James Hardinge	Petro Guy, jnr.
	Anthony Bassano	

Later, in the reign of King Charles I, in the account for the funeral of King James I, they are all together in the list of 'Musicians for windy instruments'.

The popular picture of King Henry VIII is of a Bluebeard suffering from gout. How different was the King in his youth! Since he was originally destined for the Church, music formed part of his education. We read in the Chronicles of Holinshed that in 1510 'The whole court removed to Windsor, there beginning his progresse, and exercising himselfe dailie in shooting, singing, dansing, wrestling, casting of the barre, plaieing at the recorders, flute, virginals, in setting of songs, and making of ballads; he did set two full masses, everie of them five parts, which were soong oftentimes in his chappell, and afterwards in diverse other places'. That was in the second year of his reign, and with a music-loving king we may expect to find that his musical subjects are encouraged in their art. The Royal Library at the British Museum contains some MSS of the King's music, and some of these pieces sound very well played on recorders.

At this time there lived an interesting personality, John Palsgrave by name (London c. 1480-1554). He was educated in Cambridge and Paris, and was a teacher of French. He was appointed to teach French to the King's sister, the Princess Mary, before her marriage to the French King Louis XII in 1514, and remained in her service, returning with her to England later when she married the Earl of Suffolk. In 1525 he became tutor to the Duke of Richmond, the King's bastard son. Palsgrave's chief work was a grammar and dictionary entitled *L'Esclaircissement de la Langue Francoyse, composé par Maistre Jehan Palsgrave, Angloys, Natif de Londres, et Gradué de Paris* (1530) to which we shall refer later. In 1636, more than a century afterwards, Marin Mersenne in his Harmonie Universelle tells us without mentioning any names, that an English King once sent some recorders of particular design to a French King. Does it not seem probable that he was writing about a royal wedding present—from one music-loving king to another—and is it not possible that Palsgrave was put in charge of the package (which must have been a large one)? (See page 34.)

At the time of the death of King Henry VIII an inventory of the Guarderobes was made. This MS (British Museum, Harleian 1419, dated 1547) shows that there were virginals, regals, horns and other instruments to be found in the King's various palaces, including a large collection in the charge of Philipp van Wilder, the lutenist, at Westminster. The full list of these instruments is given by Galpin and Hayes *(King's Music)*, while the flutes and recorders are listed by Welch. There were 72 flutes and 76 recorders. This list is of such special interest that we will extract the items referring to the recorders:

from the list of INSTRUMENTS OF SOUNDRIE KINDES

1. *Item* one Case wt vj recorders of Boxe in it
2. *Item* viij Recorders greate and smale in a Case couered wt blacke Leather and lined wt clothe
3. *Item* twoo base Recorders of waulnuttre one of them tipped wt Silver the same are britt redde woodde
4. *Item* foure Recorders made of okin bowes
5. *Item* vj Recorders of Ivorie in a case of blacke Vellat
6. *Item* one greate base Recorder of woode in a case of woode
7. *Item* foure Recorders of waulnuttree in a case couered wt blacke vellat
8. *Item* ix Recorders of woode in a Case of woode
   from the ADDITIONAL LIST
9. *Item* a Case couered wt crimesen vellat hauinge locke and all other garnisshementes to the same of Siluer gilte wt viij recorders of Iuerie in the same Case the twoo bases garnisshed wt Siluer and guilte
10. *Item* one case of blacke leather wt viij recorders of boxe
11. *Item* a case of white woode wt ix recorders of boxe in the same

12. *Item* a case couered wt blacke lether wt vij recorders of woode in it
13. *Item* A little case couered wt blacke lether wt iiij recorders of Iverie in it

We can learn much from this list, and to facilitate reference, numbers have been added. First of all there are the materials from which the recorders were made. In the case of 25 of them the wood was unspecified. Then there were 18 of ivory, including the two basses garnished with silver gilt. They must have been handsome instruments. Then came 23 of box-wood—always a favourite material for the turner's art. And finally there were six of walnut, including the two basses tipped with silver, and four of oak—these must have been tough to make! From the fact that they were boxed in sets, we judge that they were intended to be played together. Items 2 and 9 mention instruments of various sizes. In the case of item 9 the basses would probably not have been mentioned separately but for the silver garnishing, so it is reasonable to suppose that the other sets of four, six, seven, eight and nine were not necessarily all trebles or tenors but multiples of three and four. We shall see later that three sizes were usual, the middle one being duplicated to make up a quartet. From the use of silver, gilt and ivory these recorders must have been treasured possessions of great value to their royal owner. What happened to these instruments later, are they still in existence, and will they come to light one day? These are tantalizing questions!

The sixteenth-century saw the publication of four important books about musical instruments in Germany, Switzerland, Italy and France, which were followed by two others at the beginning of the seventeenth-century:

1. Sebastian **Virdung**: *Musica getutscht und Ausgezogen,* Strasburg and Basel, 1511
2. Martinius **Agricola**: *Musica Instrumentalis Deudsch,* Wittenberg, 1528 & 1545
3. Sylvestro **Ganassi** del Fontego: *Fontegara, la quale insegna di sonare di Flauto,* Venice, 1535
4. Philibert **Jambe de fer**: *Epitome Musical des Tons, Sons et Accordz, es Voix Humaines, Flevstes d'Alleman, Fleustes à neuf trous,*

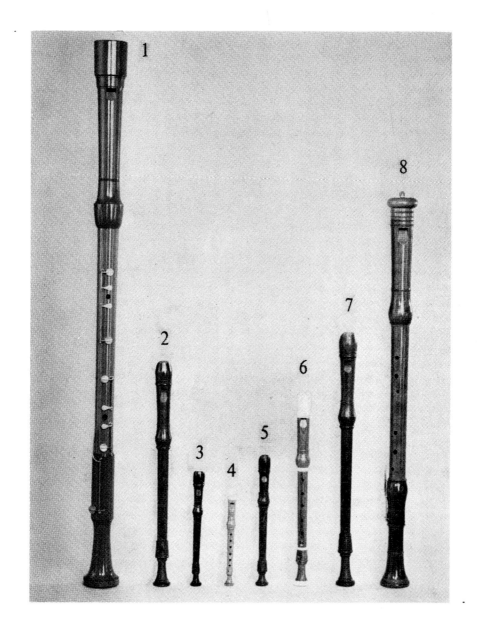

I. MODERN RECORDERS

(1) Great bass by Stieber. (2) Voice flute. (3) Sixth flute. (4) Sopranino. (5) Descant. (6) Treble. (7) Tenor, and (8) Bass by Wilhelm Herwig. Nos. 2-7 are by Dolmetsch.

II. MODERN EUROPEAN FOLK INSTRUMENTS

(1) Six-holed pipe from Norway.
(2) 'Recorder' (German fingering) from Norway.
(3) Three-holed pipe from France (Basque).

(4) Six-holed pipe from Czechoslo-vakia—the mouthpiece and lip are at the back.
(5) Five-holed pipe from Jugo-slavia, and
(6) Double pipe from Jugoslavia.

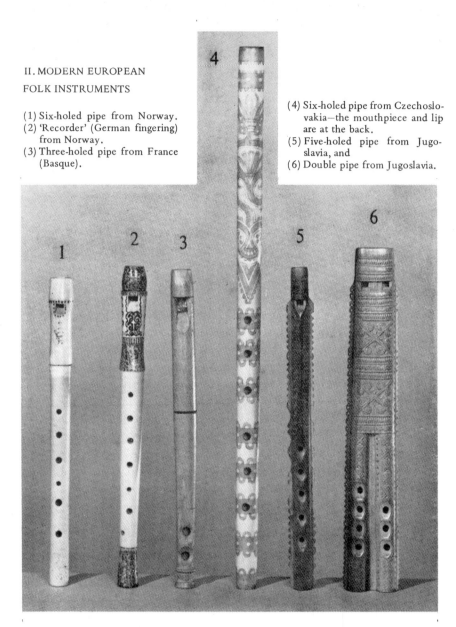

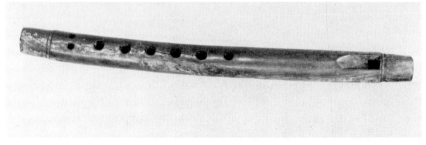

III. EARLY 15th CENTURY RECORDER — *Photo: Gemeentemuseum, The Hague*

Violes, & Violons, Lyons, 1556

5. Michael **Praetorius**:   *Syntagma Musicum*, Wittenburg, 1615-19 *De Organographia* (part 2 of the above), Wolfenbüttel, 1618-19

6. Marin **Mersenne**:   *Harmonie Universelle*, Paris, 1636

There were also two other books of a similar nature, but we are not dealing with them here as they are largely duplicates. They are: *Musurgia seu Praxis Musicae* by Ottomarus Luscinius, Strasburg, 1536, which was little more than a Latin translation of Agricola: and *Musurgia Universalis, sive Ars Magna Consoni et Dissoni* by Athanasius Kircher, Rome 1650, which followed closely the lines taken by Mersenne.

Virdung's book, like many other didactic books of the sixteenth and seventeenth centuries, is written as a dialogue between the inquiring Sebastianus and the musician, Andreas Silvanus; and begins by taking the reader through the various families of instruments with illustrative woodcuts. First there are the keyboard and stringed instruments, and then the wood-wind: Schalmey and Bombardt (double reeds). Schwegel (three-holed pipe) and Zwerchpfeiff (transverse flute). Next we come to the recorders, which are here called *Flöten*—a treble, two means and a bass (Fig. 4). It is true that there is a slight difference in size between the two mean instruments; but that is probably a little inaccuracy

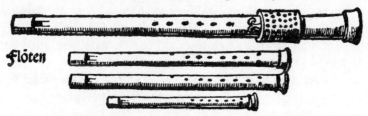

Fig. 4

in the woodcut. Then follow the Zincken and Krumhörner, brass, organs, percussion, and the instruments of the ancients. The mysteries of the rudiments of music come next, and are followed by instructions for playing the lute.

A section on the recorders occupies the last eighteen pages of the work. It will be noticed that the recorders shown in this Fig. 4 have nine holes. As the artist could not show both the front and back of the recorder in the one picture, the thumb hole is shown at the side, then there are the six holes for the first three fingers of each hand, then two holes, one on each side of the recorder. The next picture (Fig. 5) shows how these two holes are designed to suit both right- and left-handed players. The hole

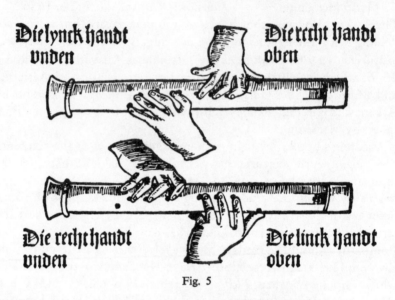

Die lynck handt vnden

Die recht handt oben

Die recht handt vnden

Die linck handt oben

Fig. 5

which was not required was plugged with wax; but this feature gave the recorder one of its French names, for, in Palsgrave's English-French dictionary (1530) we read 'Recorder—a pype—*fleute a ix neufte trous*'. In the case of the bass, the left-handed player was accommodated by having a 'butterfly touch' or 'swallow tail' to the key, so that it could be worked from either side. It will be seen that the key itself is protected by a perforated cover, or *fontanelle*, which was generally of wood and brass. The next diagram (Fig. 6) shows Virdung's numbering of the finger holes in preparation for a study of his table of fingerings (Fig. 7).

Fig. 6

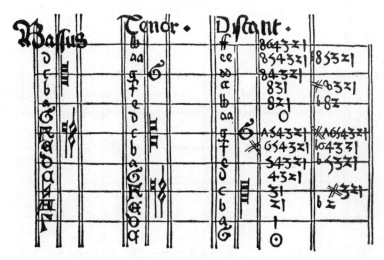

Fig. 7

This table shows that his instruments are the Bass in F, Tenor in C and Discant in G, a note higher than our modern treble. Reading the table from left to right we first have the notes of the Bass starting from Gamut—the bottom G or gamma (Γ) of the system. Actually the lowest note of the instrument is F, but Virdung could not show this as it was below the gamut. The F and C clefs are shown in their due places, and the word Bassus is firmly placed immediately above the top d to prevent players from thinking that they could get any higher notes. The Tenor notes are indicated in the same way, with the F, C and G clefs, and this is a reminder that it was usual at this period to write discant and tenor recorder parts an octave lower than the actual sound, using a suitable C clef. This instrument goes up to a b (or b flat—it is not quite clear which is intended) and the Discant in G has a similar range up to f. The two right-hand columns show the fingerings, the numbers showing the holes which have to be opened. The right-hand column fills in the flats and sharps, and a second table gives signs by which these fingerings can be indicated (Fig. 8). I have tried out Virdung's fingerings on some of the *flütes à neuf trous* in the continental museums that I have visited, and have found that in most cases they work very well.

19

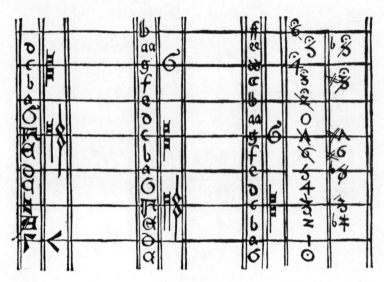

Fig. 8

The first edition of Agricola's *Musica Instrumentalis* in 1528 followed Virdung very closely, but showed four recorders of different sizes (Fig. 9), the new one being the Altus, but this does not tie up with the text which is written in terms of the three=F, C and G (like Virdung) calling the middle instrument the 'tenor-alto'*. Both Virdung and the 1528 edition of Agricola also show two little four-holed whistles, probably folk instruments, the Russpfeif and Gemsen horn (Fig. 10), the first looking like a bone instrument, the second being made from a horn, with the mouthpiece at the larger end. Now these two little instruments disappear from the second (1545) edition of Agricola, and are replaced by another little instrument, the *klein Flötlein*, which appears to be a turned-wood four-holed whistle as distinct from one made from bone or horn.

King Henry VIII was not alone in collecting large numbers of musical instruments. If we take a look at sixteenth-century Germany we will find that a catalogue was made in 1572 of the estate

*Tenor, Alt haben einerlei Art, Agricola 1545

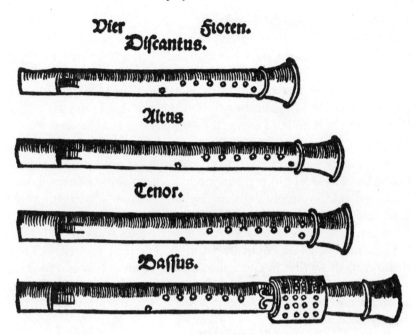

Fig. 9

of Count Raymond Fugger (1529-1569). The Fuggers were Counts of the Holy Roman Empire and international bankers of Augsburg. Their agents all over the Christian world reported to their head-quarters in frequent news-letters on political happenings, sending

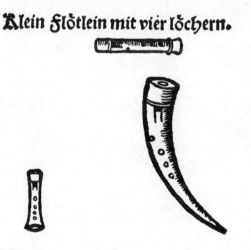

Fig. 10. The Klein Flotlein with the Russpfeif and Gemsen Horn

information that might serve their masters' purposes. This Count had possessed 111 recorders out of a total of 227 wind instruments ments. The Stuttgart Court Band in 1589 had 299 recorders out of a total of 507 wind instruments; and that at Baden in 1582 had a total of 46 recorders and 60 transverse flutes. In 1590 moving east to Graz, the list of musical instruments there again reminds one of King Henry's: here is an example:

*XXXI. Ain grosz fueteral mit flötten, darinen zwen bäsz, vier Tenor, vier discant, mer 4 klienere discäntlen und noch gar zwai klaine flötlein sampt iren geherigen mäszingen rörn oder spolleten, thuen sibenzehn stuckh, daraus ist ains verlorn.—Item ain copia newe flötten, darinen ain basz, vier tenor, zwen discänt, sambt ihren geherigen messigen spolleten; thuen sieben stuckh.

Lists such as these could be multiplied were it necessary. They all tend to show that in Germany, wind instruments predominated in the Court Bands, and that recorders *(Flöten)* were used quite as much, if not more than the transverse flutes, and were clearly distinguished from them.

Next to Venice, and the earliest known specialist book of instructions for playing the recorder, as distinct from a symposium about a number of instruments. The *Opera Intitulata Fontegara* by Sylvestro Ganassi was published there in 1535, and is generally called simply 'Fontegara', although that is probably a derivative from the name of the author's birthplace. According to Dr Hildemarie Peter, who has made a special study of this work, Ganassi was born in 1492 and was a court musician *(Sonator)* to the Doge of Venice, besides being an instrumentalist at St Mark's and a master of the viola da gamba and recorder. He also wrote a parallel treatise on the viola da gamba entitled *Regola Rubertina* (1542-43). To judge from the *Fontegara* the playing of the recorder

---

*XXXI. A big case of flutes in which are: two basses, four tenors, four discants, also four smaller discants and lastly two very small flutes (=the kleine Flötlein of Praetorius) all with their appropriate brass crooks or 'spolleten', a total of seventeen items, one of them being lost. Also a case of new flutes in which are: one bass, four tenors and two discants, with their appropriate brass 'spolleten', altogether seven items.

'Spolleten' is evidently another word for the 'crook' of the bass recorder. As the recorders probably came from Venice, it is possible that the word may have an Italian derivation, and be in some way linked with *'spoletto'*—the spindle or bobbin of a weaver's shuttle. Another possibility is that the word is used to mean 'keys' (in which case one would expect *'und'* not *'oder'*).

(which is called *flauto*) had already reached an advanced degree of technical refinement. Ganassi gives the human voice as the example to be emulated for expression and tonal variety, with due emphasis on the importance of breath control. He is sensitive to the need for different fingerings for different shades of intonation. The sixteenth-century recorder was not standardized, and Ganassi warns his reader that he must know his instrument, and be prepared to modify his fingerings for some of the high notes. In the case of the low notes he is at pains to give the fingerings which can be expected to offer the best intonation for certain particular scales. He gives the recorder a range of two octaves and a sixth—a fifth higher than the normal fingering chart. I have tried these fingerings out on a modern replica of a sixteenth-century tenor, and they work remarkably well. For articulation he uses L and R as well as the normal T, D, K and G. By far the greater part of the book is devoted to examples of divisions or variations of growing complexity, as a training for the extempore performance of such graces. In this he is more elaborate in detail than, for instance, the *Tratado de glosas sobre clausulas* of Diego Ortiz (Rome 1553) which is not so much an instruction book for the viol, but one which sets out to teach the art of playing divisons on the viol.

Is it possible to judge what success Ganassi had with the recorder in Italy? The Court Band at Florence in 1539 had three traversi, but no recorders; but in 1565, for a performance of *Psiche ed Amore* by A. Striggio sen. & F. Corteccia there were: 1 *flauto grande tenore*, 4 *flauti traverse*, 1 *traverso contralto* and 2 *flauti dritti* (or recorders). In Brussels there is a reproduction of a 'quint-bass' copied from an original at Verona. To judge by the pictures of Bartolomeo Montagna (1480-1523), Giovanni Bellini (1427-1516) and Giorgio Barbarelli di Giorgione (1478-1510), recorders were well known in Italy and were probably favourite instruments for children.

In France Philibert Jambe de Fer acknowledges a debt to Italy. In his *Epitome Musical*, after treating of music in general and singing, he allots six pages to the *fleutte d'Alleman* before coming to *Des fleuttes a neuf trouz appellées par les Italiens Flauto*. First he emphasizes the differences between the transverse flute and the recorder, and in particular the gentleness of the breath pressure required for the latter. There follows an explanation of the name *fleute a neuf trouz* and some remarks on fingering. Three pages only are devoted to the recorder before going on to the stringed instruments, but there is a table of fingerings at the end covering two octaves, and with the ninth hole shown suitably closed.

The recorder figures in two of the beautiful sixteenth-century tapestries at the Hotel de Cluny, which form part of *La Vie Seigneuriale*. In both cases the instrument is of tenor proportions and played left-handed, showing the application of the *à neuf trous* principle.

Before returning to England we must pause at Antwerp, an important centre of commerce. When in 1772 Dr Charles Burney was travelling Europe to collect material for his History of Music, he arrived in Antwerp on July 17 and spent a few days there hearing the music of the Cathedral and the various churches, and meeting the leading musicians of the city. He describes all this in the account of his travels which was published in the following year—three years before the famous History appeared. Let him tell his story:

> After this I went to a very large building on a quay, at the side branch of the Scheld, which is called the *Oosters Huys*, or Easterlings house; it was formerly used as a ware-house by the merchants trading to Lubec, Hamburg, and the Hanseatic towns; it is a very handsome structure, and has served, in time of war, as a barrack for two thousand men. I should not have mentioned my visiting this building, if I had not found in it a large quantity of musical instruments of a peculiar construction. There are between thirty and forty of the common-flute kind, but differing in some particulars; having as they increase in length, keys and crooks, like hautbois and bassoons; they were made at Hamburg, and are all of one sort of wood, and by one maker; CASPER RAVCHS SCRATEN-BACH, was engraved on a brass ring, or plate, which encircled most of these instruments; the large ones have brass plates pierced, and some with human figures well engraved on them; these last are longer than a bassoon would be, if unfolded.* The inhabitants say, that it is more than a hundred years since these instruments were used, and that there is no musician, at present, in the town who knows how to play on any one of them, as they are quite different from those now in common use. In times when commerce flourished in this city, these instruments used to be played on every day, by a band of musicians who attended the merchants, trading to the Hans towns, in procession to the exchange. They now hang on pegs in a closet, or rather press, with folding doors, made on purpose for their reception; though in the great hall

---

*The long trumpet, played lately in London, seems only to have been an ordinary trumpet straitened.

there still lies on the floor, by them, a large single case, made of a heavy and solid dark kind of wood, so contrived, as to be capable of receiving them all; but which, when filled with these instruments, requires eight men to lift it from the ground; it was of so uncommon a shape, that I was unable to divine its use, till I was told it.

One of these instruments is still to be found in Antwerp in the Vleeshuis Museum in Vleeshouwersstraat (see plate V) It is a double-bass recorder 2m 62cm in length, a wonderful relic, sans keys, sans crook, sans fontanelle; but still a testimonial to the art of the Rauch von Schrattenbach family whose mark it bears. In its prime it must have been similar to one of Mersenne's royal recorders—those which King Henry VIII probably gave to Louis XII. The lowest note of this double-bass would be 'cello C*; and it could have been made like a tenor recorder, but four times as large and four times as awkward to play. Instead, it is made twice as large as a bass recorder in F, and three additional keys extend the

range diatonically down to C 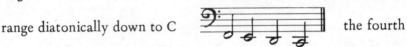 the fourth

key corresponding to the usual one for the lowest note of the bass. Whether these keys were operated by pedals as in the case of the royal instrument, we cannot say for certain, as the mechanism is lost. A replica of this Antwerp instrument, but with the keys and other fittings restored, can be seen at the Museum of the Royal Conservatoire of Music, Brussels, and there is another at the Metropolitan Museum of Art, New York. Did Burney give the maker's name correctly, or should it have been Hans Rauch von Schrattenbach, other instruments from whose workshop can be seen at the Bavarian National Museum, Munich, and at Salzburg? The Munich example, 1m 79cm long, is a great bass in C with the mark HANS RAVCH VON SCHRATT. A replica of this is also in Brussels. The Salzburg bass has the following inscription on the brass band of the fontanelle 'IHSUS MARIA ANNA 1535'.

Back in England towards the end of the sixteenth-century, music was enjoying a Golden Age under Queen Elizabeth, the Queen appropriately playing the virginals. We can imagine young men singing songs to their ladies and accompanying themselves on the lute, after-dinner parties singing madrigals, or enjoying a consort

---

*To judge from the Brussels replica this sounds nearer C-sharp, and the question arises: is this a low-pitch D or a high-pitch C?

for viols instead of a rubber of bridge. Was this the general practice, or was Thomas Morley's description of the embarrassment of Philomathes, when he had to admit he could not sing, just wishful thinking?

> But supper being ended and music books (according to the custom) being brought to the table, the mistress of the house presented me with a part earnestly requesting me to sing; but when, after many excuses, I protested unfeignedly that I could not, every one began to wonder; yea, some whispered to others demanding how I was brought up, so that upon shame of mine ignorance I go now to seek out mine old friend Master Gnorimus, to make myself his scholar. (From *A Plaine and Easie Introduction to Practicall Mvsicke* by Thomas Morley, 1597.)

In those days there was work to be done, wars to be won: the merchants of London and Bristowe were finding a new prosperity, as they opened new markets overseas. Morley's picture is probably as true to the life of those days as 'Lucky Jim' and the recorder-playing professor are to ours. True, the Court and some noble establishments went in for music in a big way, with a composer on the strength and musical servants; but was that generally so?

Music has always come into its own at times of a royal festival, a coronation or a state visit; and Queen Elizabeth's visit to Kenilworth in 1575 was no exception. The decorations which were prepared to greet her have been vividly described. On poles lining the route of her approach to the Castle there were trophies symbolic of the classical gods and goddesses; and 'on the seaventh posts, the last and next too the Castl wear thear pight too saer Bay braunchez of a four foot hy, adourned on all sides with lutes, viollz, shallmz, cornets, flutes, recorders, and harpes, as presents of *Phoebus*, the God of Muzik for rejoycing the mind, and of phizik for health to the body'. The Queen's arrival was greeted with music. A 'tune of welcum' was played by six trumpeters, then there was 'a delectable harmony of hautboiz, shalmz, cornets and such other looud muzik', and 'at the eend of the Bridge and entree of the gate, waz her Highness received with a fresh delicate armony of flutz in perfourmauns of *Phoebus* prezents'.

In Elizabethan England, wherever music was cultivated, it was of the best, and able to stand the tests of time. The madrigals and lute songs were printed, also one book of music for the virginals; but most of the latter, together with the fantasies for viols, were with a few exceptions in manuscript. We search in vain for any specific items for the recorders, and in our disappointment realize that if we make our own arrangements of other instrumental music, we are probably doing exactly what Elizabethan recorder players did. Occasionally, as in the case of Anthony Holborne's *Pavans, Galiards, Almains and other short Æirs both grave, and light in five parts, for Viols, Violins or other Musicall Winde Instruments* (London, 1599), a consort of recorders has as good a claim to a share in the title as the shawms and sackbuts, but such cases are rare. The flute part of Morley's *Consort Lessons* (London, 1599) was probably intended for a flute of the transverse kind and not a bass recorder. It may be argued that the more serious fantasias for viols were as characteristically written for those instruments as a string quartet for members of the violin family; but there remains a quantity of consort music *zeer lustich ende bequaem om spelen op alle musicale Instrumenten** such as the *Danserye* of Tielman Susato (Antwerp, 1551), *Musique de Joye* published by Jaques Moderne at Lyon in the first half of the sixteenth century and the collections of dances published in Paris in 1529 and 1530 by Pierre Attaingnant. Of even earlier date is the manuscript collection *Liber Fridoline Sichery,* in the library of the monastery at St Gall in

¶ Vingt et sept chansons musicales a quatre parties desquelles les plus cõuenables a la fleuste dallemant sont signees en la table cy dessoubz escripte par a. et a la fleuste a neuf trous par b. et pour les deux par a b. Imprimees a Paris en la rue de la Harpe deuant le bout de la rue des Mathurins prez leglise sainct Cosme par Pierre Attaingnant. Mense April. m. D. xxxiii.

Amour me poingt	a b	v	Je ne puis pas	a b	vi	Rien de bon cueur	a	viii
Amours amours	a	iiii	Jectes moy sur lherb.	a	ix	Pour q̃y dõc ne frig.	a	xiii
Allõs vng peu pl⁹ auãt	a b	v	Jamais vng cueur	a b	x	Si bon amour	a	xvi
Amour me voyant	a b	ix	Je nẽ diray mot		xiiii	Tous amoureux	a b	vii
Allez souspirs	b	xi	Je nauoys point	a	xv	Troys ieunes bourg.	b	x
De vous seruir	a b	i	Les yeulx bẽdez	a b	iiii	Va mirelidrogue		iii
Elle veult dõc	a	xi	Mirelaridon		i	Voyant souffrir	a b	xii
Gentil mareschal		iii	On dit quãmour	a b	xii	Vng petit coup		xv
Hellas amour	a b	viii	Parle qui veult	a	ii			
Hayne et amour	a	xiii	Par vng matin	a b	vii			

Superius.

Cum priuilegio ad sexenniũ   O r i

Fig. 11. Attaingnant's Chansons (1533) showing letters to indicate use of flutes and recorders.

*Pleasing and suitable for performance on all kinds of musical instruments.

Switzerland, which contains many works by the Netherlands masters, Ockeghem, Obrecht and others. Thirty-two pieces from another manuscript collection, by Wolfgang Küffer, in the Proske Library at Regensburg, have been published under the title *Carmina Germanica et Gallica*. This collection belongs to the middle of the sixteenth century and contains pieces by, among others, Othmayr, Hermann Fink, Janequin and Arcadelt. The dances of Susato, Moderne and Attaingnant are mostly quartets but benefit in performance by the addition of a drum rhythm. Attaingnant made use of a system of letters to indicate that certain of his *chansons* could be played on recorders and on flutes. The two manuscript collections are more vocal in character and are for from three to five voices. The *Pavans, Galiards* et cetera of Holborne are quintets: so also are the wonderful Pavans, Galiards and Almans in John Dowland's famous *Lachrimae* collection (London, 1605). These twenty-one pieces were originally scored for viols or violins, with an ad lib. lute part, but also sound well on recorders. Their elaborate part-writing is fascinating to the players and interesting to listen to. There are two three-part Fantasias from the Cittharn School by Holborne (London, 1597).

Even if one hesitates to adapt true madrigals for recorders by leaving out the words, many of the three-part Canzonets by Morley and Henry Youll lend themselves to such treatment. In fact the two-part Canzonets of Morley were so used as the start of the seventeenth-century. Interpolated among these vocal Canzonets are nine two-part instrumental fantasias.

By the beginning of the seventeenth century the families of instruments outlined by Virdung had grown. The three-part pattern, treble, mean and bass, had early been expanded to four parts, the mean being duplicated to take on the alto and tenor voices. But now, as often as not, a *quinta pars* was required, with even large groups for special occasions. This change can be seen in a comparison between Virdung's Musica Getutscht (1511) and the *Syntagma Musicum* (1615 and 1619) of Michael Praetorius. In the century which separated them the recorder family had grown to eight. The discant, tenor and bass of Virdung were now called alto, tenor and basset; and above them were two discants, in d" and c" respectively, and an *Exilent or Klein Flötlein* in g", while below there were a new bass in B flat and a Great Bass in E. But the

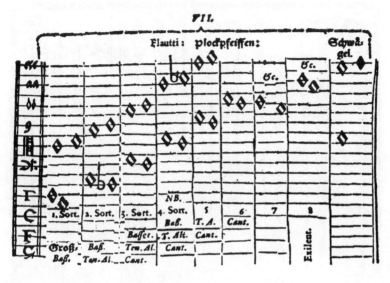

Fig. 12

three-part basis was still there, and Praetorius explained that it was customary to have groups playing together made up of adjacent instruments (Fig. 12). One such ensemble would consist of discant (d″), alto (g″) and tenor (c′), a second group of alto (g′), tenor (c′) and basset (f) and so on, down to the mellow tones of basset (f), bass (B flat) and great bass (F). He preferred the five deeper recorders 'as the small ones shriek too much, these five sound very well alone in a canzona or motet, and give a very pleasant soft harmony in a hall or room, though the largest recorders cannot be heard very well in a church'. The discant in c″ and the *Klein Flötlein* were not allotted to any of these ensembles, but their purpose may have been to serve as octave instruments to the Alto and Tenor. In the third book of his *Syntagma Musicum* Praetorius went into greater detail about methods of instrumentation and suggested ways in which different groups of voices and instruments could be contrasted in antiphonal performance: voices alone in three parts could be followed by the upper voices with a contrabass, trombone or bassoon (curtal); or the two upper parts could be accompanied by an organ or regal: or again the bass part could be sung while the two upper parts are played on two cornetti, violins or recorders.

Let us look at Plate IX from the *Theatrum Instrumentorum* with

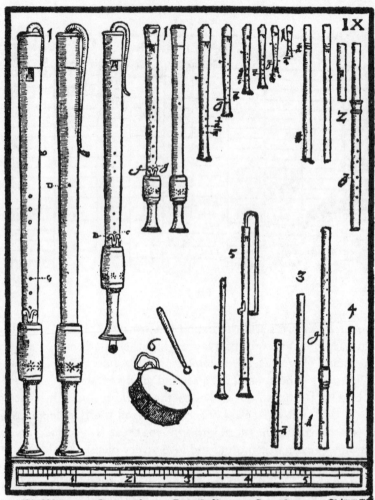

IX

ℯ. Blockflöten/ganz Stimmwerck. 2. Dolgflöt 𝔟 g. 3. Querflöten/ganz Stimwerck
4. Schweitzer Pfeiff. 5. Stamentien-Baß vnd Discant. 6. Klein Päuckän:
ju den Stamentien Pfeifflin zugebrauchen.

Fig. 13

which Book II of Praetorius's *Syntagma Musicum* concludes
(Fig. 13). Starting from the left-hand side we have the Great Consort of recorders. Elsewhere he wrote: '*Blockflöten*—latinis Fistula,
so von den Italianern Flauto, *von den Engelendern* Recordor
genennet werden', and also referred to '*der Flöten Chor* (Italis
Choro da Flauto)'. In France this would be *le grand jeu*. We have

30

front and back views of the Great Bass, showing the barrel-like fontanelle which protects the key mechanism, the swallow-tail touch of the key and the crook which enters the top of the instrument. There is one view of the bass in B flat. The little circle drawn at the lower end of the instrument is to remind us that although it flares out to form a foot, the inner bore remains small. Front and back views of the basset come next. The instrument shown has no crook. Instruments of this type were quite usual, and were blown through a hole at the back. Sometimes two smaller holes, side by side, were used. Then single examples each of the alto (g'), the two discants (c" and d") and the exilent. To the right of the figure 1 there is an even smaller instrument with three holes.

In the right-hand corner are the *Doltzflöten* which were fipple-flutes made to look like transverse flutes. Below (3) is a set of three transverse flutes (*Querflöten*) and (4) a Swiss fife *(Schweitzer Pfeiff)*. Towards the centre are treble and bass three-holed pipes and the tabor with which they would be played.

Below the picture is a scale given in old Brunswick feet. The measurements can be converted to modern terms and compared with the dimensions of actual instruments which have survived from this period. One foot on this scale approximates to eleven of our inches or about 28 cm.

Although Praetorius is writing in 1614, he is not telling his readers about new instruments but ones that were well established in his day, made and played probably fifty or sixty years earlier. In those days there were some very fine instruments in the possession of the Academia Filarmonica at Verona. A list dated 1569 mentions a chest of 22 recorders, including crooks for the three largest, and two incomplete chests. One at least of these instruments is still to be found in the Biblioteca Capitolare at Verona: a double-bass recorder 2.85 m. in length. At Schloss Ambras, not far from Innsbruck, the Archduke of the Tyrol had his castle, and an inventory of his collection of musical instruments, dated 1596, is of interest here. It mentions pipes (Pfeifen) made in Germany, others made in France, and *'ain grosse flaut per concert, von Venedig erkauft'*. ('A big flute for the consort, bought in Venice'). A basset (f) from this collection is in the Kunsthistorisches Museum at Vienna, 95.5cm. long (about 5cm. longer than the one in

Praetorius's drawing). Praetorius tells us that a Great Consort of recorders would consist of 21 instruments: 1 double bass, 2 basses, 4 Bassets, 4 tenors, 4 altos, 4 discants and two exilents, and remarks that such a set of instruments could be bought in Venice for 80 Thaler. Other collections were those of the Correr family of Venice, and of the Obizzi family at Catajo near Padua, both rich in treasures of the sixteenth century; and when they were dispersed many specimens went to Vienna, while others were acquired by Victor Mahillon for the Museum of the Royal Conservatoire of Music at Brussels. The majority of these recorders is to be found at Vienna, 39 from Catajo ranging from a sopranino (f″) 25cm. long to the double bass in G 183cm. long, stamped with the maker's mark HIE.S.

The measurements associated with the woodcut in *Syntagma Musicum* are of great value when attempting to place such instruments as those at Vienna according to their pitch and use. Pitch varied from one maker or district to another; sometimes instruments were specially made so as to be in tune with a particular church organ; but they were, as suggested by Praetorius, generally to be bought in sets. To judge from recorders of similar length to those which he illustrated the normal pitch of his day approximated to modern pitch or was only a little sharper. When we come to the period of Bach and Handel we shall find that chamber pitch is nearly a tone lower, and that in size and sound a tenor in c′ of the sixteenth century would be the same as an alto in d′ in 1700. This may seem to be little more than an antiquarian quibble, but it is of great importance when trying to reconstruct the music-making of the period. The compilers of museum catalogues help by telling us the approximate pitch in terms of the pitch of their day (French Diapason Normal c″ = 517 in most cases), and this is probably better than if they were to try to translate it in terms of sixteenth-century or one of the later pitches.

In his *Harmonie Universelle* (1636/7) Marin Mersenne suggests that the recorders should be used rather like the 4ft and 8ft registers of an organ, by having a small consort (4ft) consisting of dessus treble (f′), taille and hautcontre (tenors I and II in c′) and basse (basset in f), and a large consort (8ft) of basset, two basses (in B flat) and double bass (F). He also gives an example of recorder music, a *Gavotte pour les Flustes douces* which was composed

IV. Carved Treble from the German National Museum, Nürnberg.

Photo: German National Museum Nürnberg

VI. Bressan Treble with double holes for L.H.3 as well as R.H. 3 and 4.

Photo: Kunsthistorisches Museum Vienna.

V. Front and back views of the Great Bass by Rauch von Schrattenbach at the Vleeshuis Museum, Antwerp.
Photo: A. C. L. Bruxelles (before restoration).

VII. A CONSORT OF RECORDERS

by Hieronymus Franziskus Kynsker in the German National Museum at Nürnberg. They are: two descants in D, two trebles in G, two tenors in D and a bass in G, of boxwood stained dark, with horn mouthpieces and mounts at the joints. The bass has brass rings, and shows the swallow-tail key and fontanelle characteristic of sixteenth-century recorders. *Photo: German National Museum, Nürnberg.*

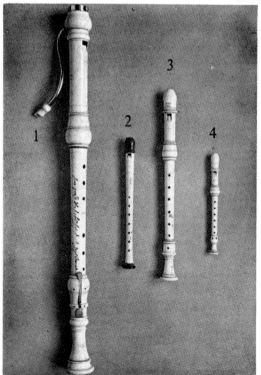

VIII. IVORY RECORDERS FROM THE BAVARIAN NATIONAL MUSEUM, MUNICH

(1) Bass recorder in F by Denner of Nürnberg.
(2) Descant in C with black mouthpiece and foot ring.
(3) Treble by Rippert.
(4) Sopranino by Rippert.
Photo: Bavarian National Museum, Munich.

Gavote pour les Fluſtes douces.

Fig. 14

for his book by le Sieur Henry le Jeune (Fig. 14), together with an *Air de Cour pour les Flustes d'Allemand* and a *Vaudeville pour les Flageollets.* It will be seen that he writes for the recorders in various C and F clefs,* but for which instruments is the little piece intended? It was Praetorius who first drew attention to the fact that recorders give the impression of sounding an octave lower than their actual pitch, and this characteristic is as true today as it was then. But that consideration does not help us to fit this piece to the instruments of Mersenne's quartet, f'-c'-c'-f. It does, how-ever, fit our present-day descant, treble, tenor and bass combination perfectly.

In Mersenne's book we find a picture of one of the 'royal flutes' to which reference has already been made (Fig. 15a). He even showed the key mechanism with the fontanelle removed (Fig. 15b).

We owe to Dr Ernst H. Meyer the discovery of three original works of the first half of the seventeenth century, which were written expressly for recorders. The first is a *Sonada a 3 Fiauti & B.C. (Basso Continuo)* from a manuscript of German or Polish origin which he found at Breslau. The work is anonymous and fits three descant (c") recorders with continuo, or descant, two trebles and continuo. But it also lends itself to 'orchestration' in the way suggested by Mersenne, by having three tenors to provide a main 8ft choir below the 4ft choir of descants. The music itself is interesting, with its changes of time, double echos and contrasts.

---

*Soprano, mezzo-soprano, alto and baritone clefs.

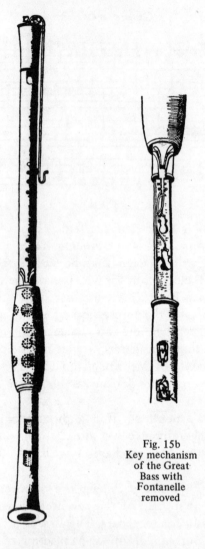

Fig. 15a
Great Bass
recorder from
Mersenne's
*Harmonie
Universelle*
(1636/7)

Fig. 15b
Key mechanism
of the Great
Bass with
Fontanelle
removed

The second is a *Sonatella a 5 Flauti et Organo* by a Venetian, Antonio Bertali (1605-1669), who was court composer and Kapellmeister to the Emperor of Austria. The manuscript was found in the St Maurice Archive at Kremsier (Kroměřiž) in Moravia, where Bertali had worked for a time at the Episcopal court. The five recorder parts are heard best on the normal sopranino, descant, treble, tenor and bass, though other groupings are possible. The style is that of a canzona, with fugued sections sand-

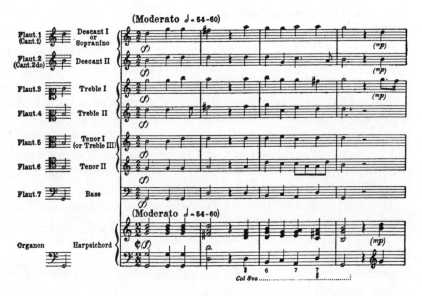

Fig. 16

wiched between sections of mainly block harmony. Another
Kapellmeister to the Imperial Court at Vienna was Johann Heinrich
Schmelzer (1623-1680) who wrote a very fine *Sonata a 7 Flauti*
(Fig. 16). One can well imagine such a work being played on a
Grand Consort of 21 recorders! With modern recorders it sounds
best on sopranino, descant, two trebles, two tenors and bass. The
form is again that of a canzona, but more extended than the
Bertali. In the central fugued sections some of the imitations are
so close as to provide many pitfalls for any inexperienced player
who essays a part! The manuscript was discovered by Dr Meyer in
the Library at Uppsala in Sweden.

Yet another work must be mentioned here, a *Sonata pro Tabula
a* 10 by H.I.F. Biber for five recorders and five stringed instruments
with a continuo. Heinrich Ignaz Franz Biber (1644-1704) was one
of the most important Bohemian composers and violinists of his
time. Today he is little more than a name even to violinists and
enthusiasts for the viola d'amore. From 1666 to 1670 he was in
the service of the Prince-Bishop of Olomouc, and it was to the
University Library there that Mr Richard Maunder traced the
manuscript which he has edited for two descants, treble, tenor and

bass recorders with two violins, two violas and violoncello.* This is an unusual work in seven short sections: Grave, Presto, Adagio, Presto (Allegro), Aria and (Allegro),† in which the first two are given to the strings, the next two to the recorders, both choirs coming together in the (Allegro)s, the Aria being antiphonal.

The recorder seems to have flourished in the Netherlands in the middle of the seventeenth century, to judge by two publications of that time. About 1646 *Der Fluyten Lust-Hof* of Jacob van Eyck was brought out in Amsterdam; and in 1654 G. van Blankenburgh's *Underwyzinge hoemen alle de Toonen de meest gebruyckelyck zyn op de Hand-Fluyt* appeared in the same city.

The brief instructions given by both van Eyck and van Blankenburgh are similar. Instead of the usual chart of fingerings, the way to play each note is described in words. These descriptions have been followed in order to produce the chart of Blankenburgh's fingerings given on page 119. It will be noticed that this chart differs from all the others in its preference for half-covering to produce the semitones, rather than the more usual cross-fingerings. It also shows a difference between, for instance, D sharp and E flat, the sharp in each case being the flatter of the two.

Fig. 17

The title page of *Der Fluyten Lust-Hof* describes Jacob van Eyck (c. 1590-1657) as *Musicyn en Directeur van de Klok-wereken tot Uitrecht* (musician and Director of the Carillon at Utrecht). He was a skilled organist and flute player, and was blind. He was paid an extra 20 guilders for entertaining 'the people walking in the churchyard with the sound of his little flute'. This *Fluyten Lust-Hof* contains about 150 pieces, most of them well-known tunes with variations. A few of the pieces are duets for two recorders.

---

* Listed by Dr Meyer in *Die Mehrstimmige Spielmusik des 17. Jahrhunderts in Nord- und Mitteleuropa* as a Sonata pro Tabula a 10 (5 Fl, 2 V., 3 Va., Org.) and indicating that the MS was in the St Maurice Archive at Kremsier. It has since been transferred to Olomouc.

†The parentheses indicate time words supplied by the editor.

The settings, which are for C instruments, give evidence of a fluent technique. The preparatory instructions show (Fig. 17) the recorder in C *(Hand-fluyt)* and *Dwars-Fluit* (transverse flute) in G. The tunes themselves stem largely from Elizabethan England: there is *Pavaen Lachrymae, Comagain* ('Come again, sweet love doth now invite') and a tune called *Rosemondt* which looks very much like our *Tower Hill, Prins Robberts Masco* (Prince Rupert's March), and so on. Psalm tunes are also used as themes for variations.

3

THE HISTORY OF THE RECORDER—PART II

About sixty miles to the west of Paris there lies the village of La Couture-Boussey in the department of Seine-et-Eure. To get there you take the Dreux Road, leaving Paris in the direction of Versailles. At Houdain (famous for its breed of poultry) you strike north-west and after a few miles find this little village.

Fig. 18. The home of the Hotteterres at La Couture-Boussey

It is now a centre of the woodwind instrument-making industry, where you will find such names as Martin, Noblet, Thibouville and others. On one side of the village green there stands the school—a broad façade behind a little avenue of trees, in the centre of which, separating the boys' school from the girls', is what might be the master's house. At the back of this is a room which serves as a museum of woodwind instruments. Many of the specimens in the glass cases were products of the workshops of this village, reminders of the days of individual craftsmanship; for this village has been a centre for this craft for over three hundred years. In the seventeenth century it was the home of the famous Hotteterre family, musicians and instrument makers. Their name figures in the *Memoires* of the Abbé de Marolles (1656). According to this writer the music-lovers of his day 'etoient ravis de la Poche et du violon de Constantin et de Bocan, de la viole d'Otman et de Maugars, de la musette de Poitevin, de la flute doûce de La Pierre et du flageolet d'Otteterre'. In the following year, there were among the musicians concerned in the ballet *Amour malade,* which was danced before the King, Obterre le père, Obterre fils ainé and Obterre le cadet. The names of many of the Hotteterres and of their relations, the Chédevilles, are to be found among the musicians of the *Grande Ecurie* of Louis XIV and XV, playing the hautbois, musette, bassoon and flute, and composing for these instruments. By far the most important contributions of the Hotteterre family to music are the improvements in the making of woodwind instruments which have been ascribed to them. During the second half of the seventeenth century they refined the hautbois to provide instruments worthy of Lully's band, *Les Douze Grands Hautbois du Roi.* The six-holed flute had hitherto been a cylindrical instrument of limited range and doubtful intonation— for this they provided a conical bore and a key for the low D sharp. Up to this time woodwind instruments had been made generally in one or at most two pieces. This meant that a fairly long piece of wood without blemishes was needed. Extra long boring tools were necessary, carrying a greater risk of inaccuracy due to 'play'. The Hotteterres are said to have given the hautboy, flute and recorder their characteristic joints, enabling their makers to use shorter lengths of wood and shorter (and more accurate) boring tools. Such improvements tended to raise the standard of instrument making, and in the case of the flute, probably provided the momentum which led to its phenomenal popularity—a popularity which carried well into the nineteenth century. It is probable that in this village of La Couture-Boussey, the baroque recorder, with its bulging joints and tapering bore (similar to that of the one-keyed flute), was evolved in time for Bach and Telemann to use to the full, and to provide the architects of our twentieth-century revival with models.

The most illustrious member of this family was Jacques Hotteterre le Romain who was probably born about 1680 and lived to about 1760. Where 'le Romain' originated is not known— it was probably acquired as a result of a visit to Italy. He joined the musicians of *la Grande Ecurie* some time before 1707, in

Fig. 19. How to hold the recorder, from 'Les Principes . . .' of Hotteterre,
Paris, 1707

which year his *Principes de la Flûte traversière ou Flûte d'Alle-*
magne, de la Flûte à bec ou Flûte douce, et du Hautbois were
published in Paris by Ballard. The importance of this method is
that it served as model for so many others—often abridged and un-
acknowledged. Hotteterre starts with the transverse flute, explaining position, embouchure, ordinary fingerings and shake fingerings.
There are folding tables for the ordinary and shake fingerings for
both the transverse flute and the recorder. Then Chapter VIII deals
with tongueing and some ornaments for the transverse flute and
other wind instruments. The ninth and last chapter of this section
deals with further ornaments. Then follows the section devoted to
the recorder. In the four short chapters the topics are again:
position (Fig. 19), ordinary fingerings, shake fingerings,
and such adaptation as is necessary of Chapter IX in the transverse
flute section. But it is interesting to notice that Hotteterre takes
into account the double holes for low F sharp and G sharp:
'Ce-pendant pour suivre les choses par ordre je parleray du *Fa*
Diézis; Il se fait en débouchant la moitié du huitième trou, sur les
Flutes qui n'ont point ce trou double: mais sur celles qui l'ont, on
débouche le plus éloigné des deux trous, ce qui se fait on retirant
le Doigt sans le lever;' and again *'Le Sol Diézis* se fait en débouch-

ant la moitié du septième trou: comme je l'ay expliqué, parlant du *Fa Diézis*; ou s'il est double, le plus éloigné'. The double holes for the F sharp are clearly shown in the pictures on the tables of fingerings. Is it not strange that more specimens of eighteenth-century recorders with these double holes have not survived? The present writer can recall only the examples by Bressan in the museums of Chester and Vienna, and another instrument at Stockholm.

In the chapter on tongueing Hotteterre uses the syllables *Tu* and *Ru*, the former being the more used. However, when double tongueing is to be employed the first two notes should be tongued with *Tu tu,* and then followed by *Ru tu ru tu*—the *Ru* coming first; and for a dotted rhythm in compound time (or in triple) he indicates *Tu tu ru* (try this in *Sellenger's Round* or the *Greensleeves* Divisions). What kind of sound is this *Ru*? The French R is surely closer to our K and G sounds than to our English R; and yet in the German Flute section of *The Modern Music Master* and in *The Compleat Tutor for the German Flute* (John Simpson, London) both of which are free translations of Hotteterre, his tongueing examples are rendered by t t r t r t and t t r *et cetera*!*

The *Principes* were Hotteterre's Oeuvre 1re. He also wrote a *Méthode pour la Musette* (Oeuvre X, 1737) and *L'Art de Préluder sur la Flûte Traversière, sur la Flûte-à-bec, sur le Haubois et autres Instrumens de Dessus* (Oeuvre VIIᵉ, Paris, 1719), besides a number of compositions in which these instruments figure.

In his preface to *L'Art de Préluder* Hotteterre explains that for him there are two kinds of Prelude. One is the composed prelude, such as might form the first movement of a suite or sonata. To this class also belong such preludes as find a place in an opera or cantata. The other is *le Prélude de Caprice* which is the true prelude, and about which he wrote his book. Of this kind of prelude he gives copious examples in a wide range of keys. As one studies the book one finds that the French violin clef (G on the lowest line) is normal for both flute and recorder, though the ordinary treble clef is often used for purposes of transposition (Fig. 20).

The first section of this book consists of *Préludes sur tous les*

---

*David Lasocki has shown, in his introduction to his translation of Hotteterre's *Principes,* that I was mistaken in thinking that the Parisian uvular R (I would call it guttural!) was normal in Molière's time. It corresponded more closely to the English R.

Fig. 20

Tons pour la Flûte Traversière. The reader is informed that many of these also fall within the compass of the *Flûte-à-bec* and are marked with a little marginal sign like the beak of a recorder. They can also be played on the oboe* if one avoids those with too many high notes! Then follows a similar series of *Traits* (or characteristic studies) *pour la Flûte Traversière* in most of the keys. Now we come to the section devoted to the *Flûte-à-bec.* This is of particular interest in that Hotteterre begins by giving arpeggios for the instrument in all the major and minor keys—at least he gives all the common chords, but qualifies this by marking *point usitez* against A flat major and minor and C sharp major and minor, while F sharp major and minor, B flat minor and E flat minor are *peu usité!* Then follow sixteen pages of *Préludes* and *Traits* for the *Flûte-à-bec.* The next section deals with the rudiments of music, with explanations of modulation, cadences, major and minor, transposition and time values, and finally two preludes with a figured bass.

The age of Louis XIV (1638-1715), and particularly the latter part of his reign and until about 1740, saw the production of quantities of suites for two treble instruments. The alternatives were many as can be judged from a typical title '. . . pour 2 Vielles, Musettes, Flûtes-à-bec, Flûtes traversières, Haubois ou Violins sans

---

*The oboe of this time had not acquired any octave keys, and was dependent on the player's skill for the octaves, which above A were difficult.

basse . . .' Now the inclusion of the musette (a polite little French bagpipe played with bellows) and the vielle (or hurdy-gurdy—a stringed instrument sounded by means of a rosined wheel) sadly cramped the scope of these little duets as far as the other alternative instruments were concerned, as both the musette and vielle have drones as well as a melody pipe/string; and the presence of drones forbids modulation, even to a related key. So the player and listener alike are condemned to successions of little dances, all in the same key! But for all their weakness those duets include some delightful little tunes, many of which have the advantage of suiting either two descants or two trebles, on account of their rather limited range.

The chief composers of the day included the Chédevilles, Naudot, Baton, Aubert and Boismortier. Many of their works bore titles such as: *Duos Galants, Babioles, Petits Concerts* and *Galanteries amusantes,* and the little dances, *La Champêtre* or *La Bergère.* For this was a time when the nobles and ladies of the court pretended to be shepherds and shepherdesses, playing on pseudo-pastoral instruments, and doing everything that shepherds and shepherdesses are supposed to do except, perhaps, keep sheep!

But, of these composers, Boismortier is head and shoulders above the rest, and when more of his music is better known his name should find a higher niche in the valhalla of musicians. Besides his quota of duets Joseph Bodin de Boismortier (1691-1755) composed six trios for three flutes *(traversières)* Op. 7, some of which have been transposed for recorders in the way suggested by Hotteterre (Fig. 20). Then there is a Concerto, *Zampogna,* for recorder, oboe and continuo, another for recorder, violin, oboe and continuo, and a set of six Concerti for five transverse flutes or other instruments.

There are suites for two recorders and continuo by La Barre the flautist and by Marin Marais the violist, as well as other works by Hotteterre. At the end of *Le Rossignol-en-amour* in his *Quatorzième Ordre* François Couperin wrote: *Ce Rossignol reussit sur la Flûte Traversière on ne peut mieux, quand il est bien joué.* ('This Nightingale should make a good flute solo—none better—if well played'). This suggestion has been followed, and with the interchange of instruments usual in eighteenth-century France, the sopranino is a possible choice, though it could be played equally well on the descant without transposition.

The French style of this period was mannered. The title of a piece often indicated the way in which it should be played; but generally the composer explained the ornaments in a preface. The student will often find that the music should be played quite differently from the way in which it is written. For instance, quavers slurred in pairs should be played 'unequally' as if changing a simple $\frac{3}{4}$ into a $\frac{6}{8}$ rhythm. What you thought was 'staccato' simply means play the quavers as written! Note that in the quotation from Hotteterre (Ex. 18) the small writing under the first Prelude reads: *Un peu animé, et crochés égales,* and under the third: *Gay, et crochés égales*—as if we ever thought of making them *inégales!* The student should consult Couperin's *L'Art de toucher le clavecin* for further information on this subject.

The recorder must have lived on in France for as long as any old instruments survived. Reading the autobiography of Hector Berlioz we find in Chapter IV: '. . . I had discovered a flageolet hidden away in a drawer, and made the most futile efforts to pick out the popular air of *Malbrouk* upon it.' and later 'I was thus a past-master on those potent and perfect instruments, the flageolet, the flute and the guitar.' In a footnote on page 20 of *The story of the Flute*, H. Macaulay Fitzgibbon wrote: ' "Le Repos" in Berlioz's *L'enfance du Christ* was originally scored for flutes-douces.' It would be most interesting to know whether Berlioz did indeed find an old flageolet in that drawer, or was it possibly an old *flûte-à-bec;* and what was Mr Fitzgibbon's authority for that interesting statement?

The innovations of the Hotteterres were not felt in England until a little time after the Restoration of the Monarchy in 1660. During the Civil War and under the Commonwealth music had suffered. Writers such as Antony à Wood have told how a few musicians used to meet in Oxford to play consorts for viols during those difficult times, and we know that Cromwell and some of his followers were fond of music. But the general climate was hostile to the arts and, even if some forms of music making survived, the consort of recorders was hard hit.

After 1660 this artistic vacuum began to be filled with new ideas from France; but before the recorder or *flûte douce* became popular, the flageolet enjoyed a vogue. Now the French flageolet, which Mersenne tells us differed from *la flûte à six trous* only in the arrangement of its finger holes, was invented by *le Sieur Juvigny*. It belonged to the same family of fipple-flutes as the recorder, but had only six finger holes. The French flageolet of the seventeenth-century had four holes in front of the fingers, and two at the back for the two thumbs. This arrangement of the holes distinguished it from all other forms of flageolet, such as the English, with six finger-holes (and no thumb hole—corresponding to the *la flûte à six trous* mentioned by Mersenne), and the double and triple flageolets of the beginning of the nineteenth-century. Another feature of the flageolet was the mouthpiece cap which was designed to contain a sponge to absorb moisture from the player's breath to prevent the instrument from blocking. The flageol or larigot, from which the flageolet got its name, is as old as the recorder, and was a folk instrument which Juvigny took and civilized.

The year 1661 saw the publication of the first edition of *The Pleasant Companion, or New Lessons and Instructions for the Flageolet* which went through a number of editions during the next seventeen years. Samuel Pepys, from whom we learn so much about London life at this time, bought a copy on April 16, 1668, and its author, Thomas Greeting, was earlier engaged by Pepys to teach his wife, for on February 28, 1666/67 he wrote:

> 'Up and there comes to me Drumbleby with a flageolet, made to suit my former and brings me one Greeting, a master, to teach my wife. I agree by the whole with him to teach her to take out any lesson of herself for £4. She was not ready to begin today, but do tomorrow.'

And then on March 1:

> 'Being returned, I find Greeting, the flageolet master come, and teaching my wife; and I do think my wife will take pleasure in it, and it will be easy for her and pleasant.'

And then, a month later:

> 'So by coach to my periwigg maker's and tailor's, and so home, where I find my wife with her flageolet master, which I wish she would practise.'

And on May 8, 1667:

> 'And so home to dinner, where I find my wife's flageolette master and I am so pleased with her proceeding, though she hath lost time by not practising that I am resolved for the encouragement of the man to learn a little myself for a month or so, for I do forsee if God send my wife and I to live, she will become very good company to me.'

Samuel Pepys himself was an old hand at the flageolet for references to it abound right from the start of the Diary, such as this, for February 17, 1659/60:

> 'And so went to Mr. Gunning's to his weekly fast, and after sermon, meeting there Monsieur L'Impertinent, we went and walked in the park till it was dark. I played on my pipe at the Echo, and then drank a cup of ale at Jacob's. So to Westminister Hall, and he with me.'

The recorder did not come into Pepys's Diary until 1667/8. On February 27 in that year he went to see a revival of Massinger's play *The Virgin Martyr*. He had already seen it about seven years previously, but did not think much of it on that occasion; but this time it made a great impression on him:

> 'With my wife to the King's house, to see 'The Virgin Martyr', the first time it hath been acted a great while: and it is mighty pleasant; not that the play is worth much, but it is finely acted by Beck Marshall. But that which did please me beyond any thing in the whole world was the wind-musique when the angel comes down, which is so sweet that it ravished me, and indeed, in a word, did wrap up my soul so that it made me really sick, just as I have formerly been when in love with my wife; that neither then, nor all the evening going home, and at home, I was able to think of any thing, but remained all night transported, so as I could not believe that ever any musique hath that real command over the soul of a man as did this upon me: and makes me resolve to practice wind-musique, and to make my wife do the like.'

And a few days later:

> 'To the King's house to see 'The Virgin Martyr' again, which do mightily please me, but above all the musique at the coming down of the angel, which at this hearing the second time, do still commend me as nothing ever did, and the other musique is nothing to it.'

Pepys was very busy at this time, but this 'winde-musique' must have been continually on his mind until, on April 8:

> 'With Lord Brouncker to the Duke of York's playhouse, where we saw 'The Unfortunate Lovers', no extraordinary play, methinks, and thence to Drumbleby's, and there did talk a great deal about pipes; and did buy a recorder, which I do intend to learn to play on, the sound of it being, of all sounds in the world, most pleasing to me.'

It may be remarked *en passant* that the personality of Drumbleby has puzzled students for some time. Nobody has ever found a recorder or flageolet from his workshop, but Eric Halfpenny's researches at the Guildhall Library have been rewarded with the information that he was born about 1634, son of Thomas Drumbleby, a spectacle-maker of London, was bound apprentice to William Shaw (April 3, 1648) and became a Freeman of the Turners' Company on April 5, 1655.

How interesting it would be if Pepys had recorded for us his discussion with Drumbleby. But, no: we are left to guess. Pepys was a frequent theatre-goer, accustomed to the normal theatre music of his day, and he already played the flageolet. What new sound could he have heard that had this strange effect on him? From the fact that there and then he bought a recorder, and his opinion of that instrument's tone quality, it is most reasonable to assume that it was a consort of recorders that he heard. What was new about that? Only that they might have been the new *flûtes douces,* which looked and sounded different from the earlier types—instruments made in the three joints and with the characteristic bulges and turnings which we now take for granted, but which probably originated with the Hotteterres of La Couture-Boussey.

If what Pepys heard at the King's house was a consort of recorders, the instruments may have been the latest thing from France, but the music on that occasion was following a convention of dramatic music which had been established from Elizabethan times: trumpets for war, horns for the hunt, a fiddle for a wedding, and so on. Recorders were deemed appropriate for a number of dramatic occasions which could, at first, be classed under the headings: 1) Funerals and 2) The Supernatural (appearances of gods, goddesses or angels, or other miraculous happenings); and later on: 3) Love Scenes, 4) Pastorals, and 5) Imitations of Birds.

John Manifold gives four examples of this association of music for recorders with funerals, from stage directions. We shall find the same associations when we come to discuss Bach's use of the recorder. The following quotation from *The Broken Heart* will serve as an example:

> Stage direction from V, iii: 'A Temple. An altar covered with white; two lights of virgin wax upon it. Recorders play, during which enter attendants bearing Ithocles on a hearse, in a rich robe with a crown on his head, and place him on one side of the Altar. After which, enter Calantha, crowned and attended . . . Calantha kneels before the altar, the Ladies kneeling behind her, the rest stand off. The recorders cease during her devotions. Soft music.'

But Mr. Pepys's 'Winde-musique' belongs to our second category, the supernatural, and here there are a number of parallels; for example Dryden in *Albion and Albanius:*

> Stage Direction: 'A Machine rises out of the sea; it opens and discovers Venus and Albanius sitting in a great scallop-shell richly adorned. Venus is attended by the Loves and Graces, Albanius by Heroes; the shell is drawn by dolphins; it moves forward while a Symphony of flutes-doux, etc. is playing, till it lands them on the stage, and then it closes and sinks.'

Another stage direction, this time from *Bonduca*, reads:

> 'A Temple of the Druids . . . Music. Enter in solemnity the Druids singing . . . Bonduca, Caratach, Nennius and others, (and, after sacrifice and prayers) Exeunt. Recorders playing.'

In Purcell's music for this play, recorders accompany the duet (for two Priestesses) 'Sing, ye Druids, sing'. In an earlier example, when Emilia sacrifices to Diana, in *Two Noble Kinsmen,* the stage direction reads 'Still music of records'.

To understand these conventions and to appreciate their appropriateness, one must try to imagine the timbre of a consort of recorders, and the effect it can produce in contrast to the sounds of other instruments. Imagine some music played by a string orchestra, probably with the additional colour of oboes or trumpets, or both, and then a few chords played by the recorders. By contrast the recorders will sound cool and other-worldly, and in *The Virgin Martyr* this gentle, cool sound would undoubtedly enhance the wonder at the appearance of the angel, or in some other play or masque, at the approach of the goddess.

Then one might ask, how is it that this cool sound is also to be regarded as appropriate to our third category of love scenes? Look at a Venus by Titian. How 'cool' is the texture of her skin—and yet, in contrast with the rich draperies of the rest of the picture, how sensual. In this same way the tone of the recorders seem to present music *au naturel*. These two appropriatenesses, the other-worldly and the amorous, are as close as religion and sex would seem to have been to the writer of *The Song of Songs*.

The fourth category, the pastoral use of the recorders, probably came over from France. It is easy to explain: the shepherd's pipe, the portable instrument with which he passes the time while tending his sheep, although in fact more probably a bagpipe or simple reed instrument, can be figuratively a flute of some kind, and so a

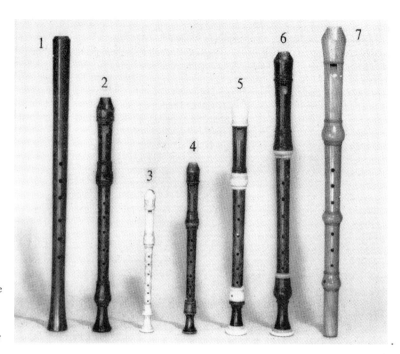

IX. FROM THE WRITER'S COLLECTION

(1) Replica of 16th-century tenor: original in the Dayton Miller Collection.
(2) Treble by Wijne of Nijmegen.
(3) Sixth flute by Stanesby Junior.
(4) Fourth flute by Bressan.
(5) Treble by Bressan. (6) Voice flute by Hail, and (7) Replica of Tenor by Stanesby: original formerly in the possession of Dr J. C. Bridge. Nos. 1 and 7 are replicas by Rudall, Carte and Co., London.

X. A recorder player of the eighteenth-century. Detail of an engraving from *The Modern Music Master* (c. 1731). From a copy in the writer's library.

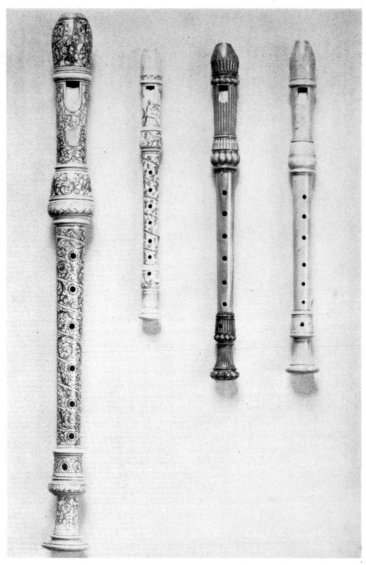

XI. Four ivory recorders from the Dayton Miller Collection, Library of Congress, Washington, U.S.A. 945. Treble, maker unknown, engraved with spiral design of leaves, flowers, fruit and birds. This recorder is in six separate pieces: head (two parts which screw together), body and foot (3 pieces including the ring which screws on at the lower end). 1259. Sopranino, maker unknown, engraved with spiral design of birds, lion, horse, deer, snake, man playing double pipes and grape vine spiralled round the instrument. 1257. Sixth flute, carved by W. Beukers (c. 1704, Amsterdam?). 1214. Sixth flute by T. Stanesby (c. 1668-1734) *Photo: Library of Congress, Washington.*

(These instruments are shown from left to right: the numbers refer to the list of the collection.)

recorder. It might be argued that an oboe might give as true a representation (cf. Handel's Pastoral Symphony in the *Messiah*).

The fifth group—imitations of birds—is also obvious. Here we must mention another use of the flageolet. These little instruments were made in different sizes; and the smallest, the bird flageolet, was used in the eighteenth-century in order to teach singing birds to sing little tunes. In 1717 Richard Meares published a little book called *The Bird Fancyer's Delight* which gave *directions concerning the teaching of all sorts of singing-birds, after the flageolet and flute, if rightly made as to size and tone.*

Owing to a tradition of versatility amongst wind players, the introduction of a group of recorders for a special effect did not necessarily mean the engagement of extra players. Frequently the recorder parts, in this period marked Flute, *Flauto* or even *Fluto*, were written into the oboe parts. The wind players would just put down their oboes and pick up their recorders, changing back afterwards.

The use of recorders in this way was confirmed in the music of Henry Purcell (1659-1695), the greatest composer of this age. Purcell left no solo music for our instrument, and only one piece which could be described as chamber music for recorders, but his use of them in his dramatic works and odes is always significant. One might say that he arrived on the musical scene at the right time to welcome and introduce these new recorders. On leaving the Chapel Royal when his voice broke, in 1673, he was appointed:

'keeper, maker, mender, repayrer and tuner of the regalls, organs, virginalls, flutes and recorders and all other kind of wind instruments whatsoever, in ordinary, without fee, to his Majesty, and assistant to John Hingston, and upon the death or other avoydance of the latter, to come in ordinary with fee.'

His first important use of the recorders was in the incidental music for *Theodosius* (1690), a spectacular play,* produced at the Duke's Theatre, in which they make two appearances, being particularly effective in 'Prepare, the rites begin' in the ritual scene. This belongs to our second class of dramatic occasions, together with the duet from *Bonduca* (1695) already mentioned. Our third class,

---

*In *The Spectator*, No. 92, for Friday, June 15, 1711, the subject of which is the choice of a library for a lady: 'Plays of all sorts have their several advocates; . . . Theodosius, or the Force of Love, carried it from all the rest'.

Two in one upon a Ground.

Chaconne for Flutes, in the Third Act.

Fig. 21

of love scenes, includes 'In vain the amorous flute' from the 1692 *Ode for St Cecilia's Day* and 'One charming night' from *The Fairy Queen* (also 1692). 'Shepherds, shepherds, leave decoying' *(King Arthur*, 1691) obviously belongs to the fourth class. In this the recorders join those other pastoral instruments, the oboes, with a gay introduction to the duet. The fifth class is wonderfully represented by 'Hark, how the songsters of the air' in *Timon of Athens* (1694). There are many more places where the recorders are displayed like musical gems, such as 'the bashful Thames' from *The Yorkshire Feast Song* (1690) and 'Strike the Viol' from *Come, ye sons of Art* (1694); but we must make special reference to the Chaconne 'Two in one on a Ground' which follows the Second Act Tune in *Dioclesian* (1690). This is a canon between the two recorders over a ground bass—one of the most beautiful pieces ever written for them. *Dioclesian* was a spectacular version of Beaumont and Fletcher's *The Prophetess*, in which the recorders had already appeared twice; in 'Charon the peaceful Shade', and a gay song for counter-tenor, 'Since the toils and the hazards of War's at an end'.

On most occasions when Purcell uses the recorders, it is to provide an obbligato accompaniment to the voice, with, of course, the continuo. In this we are reminded of the entry in John Evelyn's diary for November 20, 1679:

> 'I dined with Mr. Slingsby, Master of the Mint, with my wife, invited to hear music, which was exquisitely performed by four of the most renowned masters: Du Prue, a Frenchman, on the lute; Signor Bartholomeo, an Italian, on the harpsichord; Nicholao on the violin; but, above all, for its sweetness and novelty, the *viol d'amore* of five wire strings played on with a bow, being but an ordinary violin, played on lyre-way, by a German. There was also a *flute douce*, now in much demand for accompanying the voice. Mr. Slingsby, whose son and daughter played skilfully, had these meetings frequently in his house'.

Purcell's solitary chamber work for recorders is another Chaconne for three trebles over a ground bass.* This exists in a copyist's hand (Brit. Mus. R. M. 20. h. 9) as for three violins and continuo, with a note which reads: 'play two notes higher for F(lutes)'. There is every reason to suppose that the flute version was the original one which the copyist had transposed down for the violins.

Surveying Purcell's use of the reocrders, we find that he almost always used them in pairs—two trebles—though there is some evidence that a bass recorder was used for at least one performance of the 1692 *Ode for St Cecilia's Day*. Furthermore, after hearing and performing in several of these works, the impression remains that Purcell was particularly fond of the recorders and of the qualities they could bring to his music.† This impression is emphasized by the fact that recorders figure prominently in the three odes written to honour his death, by his friends Dr John Blow, Jeremiah Clarke and Henry Hall respectively.‡ It is true that there was the association of the cool tone of the recorders with the cold hand of death; but it is as if these three composers knew that Purcell was as fond of the sound of the recorder as he was of the counter-tenor voice.

One of the most astonishing effects in music is to be found in

---

*Discovered by Mr Layton Ring.

†For a fuller discussion, see Dr Walter Bergmann's *Henry Purcell's use of the Recorder* in Hinrichsen's Eleventh Music Book; Music-libraries and Instruments'.

‡see 'Three Pieces of Music on Henry Purcell's Death' by Walter Bergmann in *The Consort*, July 1960.

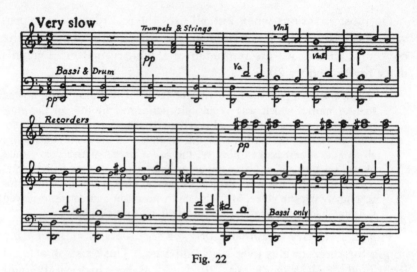

Fig. 22

Jeremiah Clarke's piece which includes an instrumental number entitled *Mr. Purcell's Farewell*. The poignant insistence of the recorders sends a chill down the hearer's spine (Fig. 22).

A number of Henry Purcell's contemporaries made notable use of the recorder: his brother Daniel Purcell, Dr Blow, Godfrey Finger, John Banister, and James Paisible. Besides his *Ode on the Death of Henry Purcell* which is scored for two counter-tenors, two treble recorders and continuo, Blow makes important use of the recorders in the Maske *Venus and Adonis*. Here they are used, not for the Prologue with its chorus of shepherds and shepherdesses but for the first act, where *The Curtain opens and discovers Venus and Adonis sitting together upon a Couch, embracing one another*, combining classes 2 and 3 of our appropriate dramatic occasions!

Daniel Purcell (c. 1660-1717) composed some attractive sonatas for treble recorder and continuo. In one set of six published by Walsh he collaborated with Finger, each contributing three sonatas. Another similar publication consists of three solo sonatas and three trio-sonatas for two treble recorders and continuo. There is also a duet for two trebles. Godfrey Finger, who collaborated with him on more than one occasion, was a Moravian who settled in England and enjoyed royal patronage and some measure of popularity until in 1700, when he received only the fourth prize for a setting of *The Judgement of Paris*. This so offended him that he left England and secured an appointment to the Queen of Prussia. Besides the

Fig. 23. A Consort of Recorders from Hudgebut's *Thesaurus Musicus* (1693)

three solo sonatas already mentioned, he composed a number of duets for two treble recorders and a trio-sonata for recorder, oboe and continuo.

James Paisible, who lived in London during the latter part of the seventeenth-century and beginning of the eighteenth, was head of the King's Band of Music from 1714-1719. He was probably a Frenchman and we find him nominating his 'good friend Peter Bressan', the instrument maker, as his executor in 1720. In 1675 we find his name at the head of the list of *French violins and hoboyes* of his Majesty's Musick, playing for a Maske at Whitehall. His compositions include a set of six duets for two trebles, Op. 1, some of which also appear in another version as trio-sonatas for two trebles and continuo. A number of his little duet movements appear in John Hudgebut's *Thesaurus Musicus* (1693-1696), and there is a crisp little sonata for four treble recorders and continuo.

We have noted the duet-sonatas for treble recorders by Daniel Purcell, Finger and Paisible. This seems to have been a very popular form, and these pieces were no doubt written to suit the capabilities of the amateur recorder players of the time. Two other composers of these sonatas were Raphael Courteville and Dr William Croft (1678-1727) the organist, who also composed a Cantata 'Celladon' for soprano voice, treble recorder and continuo—a charming pastoral.

Hudgebut's *Thesaurus Musicus,* to which we have just referred, seems to have been a kind of magazine of music—of songs and little duets for recorders. Among the other contributors to the duets were Robert King and John Banister (1630-1679), both members of the King's Band.

Banister seems to have been a versatile musician, for Pepys records:

> 'Comes and dines with me W. Howe, and by invitation Mr. Harris and Mr. Banister, most extraordinary company both, the latter for musick of all sorts, and the former for everything: here we sang, and Banister played on the theorbo, and afterwards on the flageolet'. (March 29, 1667/8.)

He led the royal violins until 1666 when (December 24) there was and 'Order that Mr. Banister and the 24 violins . . . obey the directions of 'Louis Grabu'. In 1681 Banister published a little book entitled *The Most Pleasant Companion; or, Choice New Lessons for the Recorder or Flute* evidently intending to be one up on Greeting and his *The Pleasant Companion . . . for the Flageolet!* Two years earlier John Hudgebut had brought out *A Vade Mecum for the Lovers of Musick, Shewing the Excellency of the Rechorder* which must have been the first of a long line of little books of instructions and tunes. It also brought to the fore the rivalry between the flageolet and the recorder as the following quotation from his preface will show:

> '. . . Of Instruments (though there be several species) there is none which comes nearer in Imitation to the Voice (which is the Design and Excellency of all Musick) than that which we call Wind Instruments, as the Flagilet, Rechorder, &c. as taking its inspiration, immediately from thence, and naturally dissolving into the same. Of these, though the Flagilet like Easau hath got the start, as being of a more Antient standing the Rechorder like Jacob hath got the Birth-right, being much more in Esteem and Veneration, with the Nobility and Gentry, whilst the Flagilet sinks down a Servant to the Pages and Footmen.
>
> But we do not design in lessening the Flagilet to exalt the Perfections of the Rechorder: we will allow the Flagilet all its just attributes, and see if the Rechorder do not equal or excel them.
>
> The Flagilet is a good Companion being easily carried in the Pocket, so is the Rechorder: The Flagilet is always in Tune so is the Rechorder: Besides the Sweetness of the Sound, which is much more Smoother and Charming, and the Extent and Variety of the Notes, in which it much excells the Flagilet.
>
> As all Instruments have found great access as well as Improvements in this Nation, this of the Rechorder hath not found the least encouragement, being into the favour of Ladies, and made the Gentleman's Vade Mecum.

Of this success and good Entertainment of the Rechorder I have attempted to shew my zeal for its improvement, hoping all Ingenious Gentlemen will pardon the deficiency of the performance, considering it is the first Essay of this kind: . . .'

After Hudgebut and Banister, the next of these little books was *The Genteel Companion; Being exact Directions for the Recorder . . . Carefully Composed and Gathered by Humphry Salter,* which was published by Richard Hunt and Humphry Salter in 1683. Then came:

1684: 1686   John Carr: The Delightful Companion: or, Choice new lessons for the Recorder or Flute

c. 1690   The Compleat Flute-Master: or, The whole Art of playing on ye Rechorder (published by Walsh and Hare)

1706   The Flute-Master, Compleat, Improved (John Young)

The pattern of these Companions and Flute-Masters was to give, first of all, the fingerings and then a selection of popular tunes. They borrowed from the flageolet the method of dot notation in which the fingerings were shown by means of little dashes on a six-lined staff—a form of tablature in which signs indicating the rhythm were placed over the fingerings. In the case of the recorder, more lines were needed—usually seven, or eight for the fingering table—and the tunes were given in staff notation as well. Soon the tablature disappeared except for the table of fingerings, and

Fig. 24. From Humphry Salter's *Genteel Companion* (1683)

55

elaborate instructions were added for transposing tunes to more suitable keys. There were also explanations of the signs for the various 'graces'; the 'shake', 'beat' or 'sweetening', 'double relish' and the rest. Then in 1707 came the publication in Paris, of Hotteterre's *Principes de la Flûte traversière . . . de la Flûte à bec ou Flûte Douce . . .* which was to influence so many later publications.

It will be noticed that at this time the name of our instrument was uncertain. Sometimes it was the Rechorder, at others the Flute: French influences made it the *Flûte douce* or *Flûte à bec*. In the British Museum there is a little volume of *Airs for the Flute* published in Edinburgh (1735) by Alexander Baillie, in which it is called the *Flûte à Beque*. The name 'Recorder' was fast disappearing and the instrument was generally *Flauto* or Flute, and was soon to become the 'Common Flute' while the simple title of Flute was returned to the Transverse or German type.

4

THE HISTORY OF THE RECORDER—PART III

Just as a candle is often brightest immediately before it dies, so the recorder enjoyed its greatest popularity just before it was replaced by the German flute, and rendered obsolete for about a century and a half. To understand this we must look at the rival instrument, the German flute or traversière.

There were six-holed side-blown flutes side by side with recorders with eight holes (or *neuf trous*) as far back as we can seek and further. Henry VIII had both, so had Virdung, Agricola, Jambe de Fer, Praetorius, Mersenne and the rest. But they were cylindrical instruments and lacked the niceties of tone and intonation which could be claimed for the recorders; nor was it possible to make and play bass traversi comparable to the bass and larger recorders. The largest flute shown by Praetorius was a mere three foot six inches long as compared with his double bass recorder of twice that length. A larger flute would have been impossible to play unless the head could be turned round to bring it nearer to the player. Mersenne had already made a suggestion that key mechanism should be added to the flute, but the idea was not taken up until about a hundred and fifty years later. But the modifications made by the Hotteterre family were to influence the whole pattern of music. It was probably about 1650 that they introduced the jointed instrument with a conical bore, and about twenty years later they provided it with the key for the lowest semitone—the D sharp key. Hotteterre le Romain's *Principes de la Flûte Traversière* provided the instructions; he, La Barre and others played it and made it known in musical circles. Buffardin took the new flute to Dresden, while the man who introduced it to English audiences and musicians was John Loeillet.

Endless confusion has surrounded the personality of this Loeillet. On the one hand, a great deal of music has been attributed to him: on the other, that music has had to be divided between three Loeillets.* It all started because the Loeillet family

---

*Brian Priestman has most ably unravelled the tangle in *The Consort*, No. 11, and in *Musik in Geschichte and Gegenwart;* and his researches are further confirmed by Professor Alec Skempton who has unearthed the will of John Loeillet, in which he refers to his brother in Munich.

favoured for their children the initials J. and J. B. The family home was Ghent, and there were at least three musicians—composers and performers—named Loeillet: (1) Jean Baptiste of Lyons (1688-) who described himself on his published works as 'de Gant' to link himself with the family home; a cousin (2) Jacob Jean Baptiste or Jacques (1685-1748), who was city oboeist at Ghent in 1702, but moved on to Brussels and Munich, and eventually to Paris where some sonatas of his were published chez Boivin; and his brother (3) Jean Baptiste (1680-1730) who became our John of London. J. B. (1) of Lyons published a number of sonatas for recorder and continuo with Roger of Amsterdam, most of which were later brought out again (pirated?) by Walsh in London. Jacques's music has not been republished in modern editions, unless the quintet referred to below is his. John's (3) works were mainly trio-sonatas including a number for recorder, oboe and continuo, and were published by Walsh, though the first opus was brought out by Wright of London before John Baptiste had been anglicized to John. The fact that the name L'Oeillet or Loeillet sounded rather like Lully (another J. B.) caused further confusion, and some little harpsichord pieces by Loeillet were printed in *The Modern Music Master* (c. 1731) as by Mr Lully.

In the past, the music of the Loeillets has suffered at the hands of editors who have arranged their music for instruments other than those intended by the composers. Recorder sonatas (by J.B. of Lyons) have appeared two octaves lower for the 'cello, while some trio sonatas by John of London have been converted into solo sonatas, the second instrumental part providing a tune for the pianist's right hand. In fact most musicians of the writer's generation first met the music of 'Loeillet' in the distorted editions of Alexandre Beon, and only in recent years has it become possible to know something of the solo sonatas of J. B. of Lyons and the trio sonatas of John of London.

There is an interesting Quintet in B minor by one of the Loeillets which has been edited by Rolf Ermeler from a copy in the Library at Rostock. This is scored for the unique combination of two traversi, two voice flutes and continuo. The original notation of the voice flute parts is in D minor and this, if played quasi treble recorder, sounds on the voice flute in B minor.

The editor remarks that the names *Flauto di voce* or *Flûte de voix* are not known in Germany. The voice flute is clearly an alto in D, an octave below the Sixth Flute, of which many eighteenth-century examples exist. As to which of the Loeillets it should be ascribed; Jacques, who travelled in Germany, seems more likely than the Jean Baptiste (of Lyons) to whom the editor gives the work.

John Loeillet came to London about 1705 and became principal flautist at the Queen's Theatre in the Haymarket (known as the King's Theatre from 1714-1837). As the result of changes at the theatre in 1710 he left to devote himself to teaching the harpsichord and flute, in which he was eminently successful, and to concert giving. At his house in Hart Street, Covent Garden (now known as Floral Street) it is said that the music of Corelli was first heard in London. It is also said that at his death he left a fortune of £16,000.

The influence of John Loeillet must have been great. He arrived to introduce the new flutes, reaping the benefits of their growing popularity as a teacher, also playing a pioneer part as a concert-giver. If we except the fanfares of state occasions and the music of the court, instrumental music, up to this time, had been an affair of personal participation at home, or the accompaniment to the dance or drama. The idea of going to a concert in a large concert-hall was unknown, and in fact the idea of a concert as a two-sided affair with performers and audience was only just emerging. Other things that were new in music at the end of the seventeenth century were dynamic contrasts and a more dramatic expression. Roger North expressed this change in his autobiography, *The Autobiography of The Hon. Roger North* edited by Jessopp, London, 1887, when describing his grandfather's music parties:

> '. . . For more important regale of the company, the concerts were usually all viols to the organ or harpsichord. The violin came in late and imperfectly. When all hands were well supplied, then a whole chest went to work, that is six viols, music being formed for it, which would seem a strange sort of music now, being an interwoven hum-drum, compared with the brisk *battuta* derived from the French and Italian.'

And again, when describing the 'old English music':

> 'It is not like a hurry of action, as looking on at a battle, where the concern for one side or other makes a pleasure, but like sitting in a pleasant cool air in a temperate summer evening, when one may think

59

or look or not, and still be pleased. At length the time came off the French way and fell in with the Italians and now that holds the ear. But still the English singularity will come in and have a share.'

The idea of the public concert seems to have originated with John Banister, for in the *London Gazette* of December 30, 1672, there appeared the following announcement:

'These to give notice, that at Mr. John Banister's house (now called the musick school) over against the George Tavern, in White Fryers, near the back gate of the Temple, this Monday, will be Music performed by excellent masters, beginning precisely at 4 of the clock in the afternoon, and every afternoon for the future, precisely at the same hour'.

Roger North corroborates this in his *Memoires of Musick:*

'He (Banister) procured a large room in Whitefryers, neer the Temple back gate, and made a large raised box for the musitians, whose modesty required curtaines. The room was rounded with seats and small tables alehouse fashion. 1s. was the price and call for what you pleased. There was very good musick, for Banister found means to procure the best hands in towne, and some voices to come and performe there, and there wanted no variety of humour, for Banister himself (inter alia) did wonders upon a flageolet to a thro-base, and severall masters had their solos.'

The idea grew and the promoters of concerts soon realized that the larger the room, the greater the audience and the greater the financial reward! And so it came about that instruments of stronger tone and, at the same time, capable of a wider range of expression, were needed. Although spinets were still needed at home, the concert harpsichord became more elaborate. The sprightly violins were already replacing the viols, though the bass viol lingered on. Recorders could not give the wider range of dynamics that was demanded as readily as could the new flutes. So the former were gradually to be replaced by the latter.

If you blow more strongly to get a loud note on a recorder, you will also get a sharp note, unless you make some compensating change of fingering. Similarly a soft note would be flat. On the transverse flute the player can make the necessary compensation by means of a lip adjustment; and it was this greater flexibility of tone which recommended the new flute to the builders of the new orchestra. About 1714, while John Loeillet was teaching the recorder and other instruments in London, an Englishman, Robert

Valentine, was in Rome. Biographical details are sadly lacking, but he seems to have been a violinist and composer who later, about 1730, appeared in London as a flute player. On some publications he is known as Robert Valentine of Rome, and on others as Roberto Valentino *Inglese*. His music, which includes a number of solo sonatas for flute (recorder) and continuo, and trio sonatas for two flutes and continuo, seems to have been very popular.

A much more popular figure among recorder players came a little later. He was Johann Christian Schickhard of Hamburg, who flourished about 1730 and composed sonatas for the new German flutes as well as the recorder.

Sir John Hawkins never lost an opportunity to scoff at the recorder and wrote (having a dig at the little books of instructions): 'And to come nearer to our own times, it may be remembered by many now living, that a flute was the pocket companion of many who wished to be thought fine gentlemen. The use of it was to entertain ladies, and such as had a liking for no better music than a song-tune, or such little airs as were then composed for that instrument; and he that could play a solo of Schickhard of Hamburg, or Robert Valentine of Rome, was held a complete master of the instrument . . .'

Besides the more conventional solo sonatas, including a series of twenty four in all the major and minor keys, Schickhard composed an unusual set of Concerti for four treble recorders and continuo. Some movements have the brittle texture of Paisible's work for the same instruments, others have the weight of a concerto grosso. There are interesting clashes in the harmony, though it is sometimes difficult to know whether they are intended effects (like some of Purcell's) or simply carelessnesses of writing! He is said to have arranged Corelli's Concerti for recorders, and Walsh and Hare advertised:

> 'Corellis XII Concertos Transpos'd for Flutes viz a Fifth a Sixth a Consort and Voice Flute. The proper Flute being nam'd to each Concerto and so adapted to the Parts that they perform in Consort with the Violins and other Instruments. Throughout the Whole being the first of this kind yet publish'd.'

As we shall learn (page 65) from Tans'ur, recorders were made in many different sizes, but that the treble recorder or 'consort flute' as it was then called, was regarded as the basic instrument, those in other keys being treated as transposing instruments. What we now call the descant recorder was the fifth flute, a little descant in D was the sixth flute, while the octave flute or *flauto piccolo* was what we now call the sopranino in F. There were also the fourth flute in B flat and the voice flute in D, an octave below the sixth flute.

Of these the sixth flute was a very popular solo instrument, one for which three composers wrote concerti: Robert Woodcock, John Baston, and William Babell. Of Woodcock's six recorder Concerti three are for a solo sixth flute while the other three are for two sixth flutes. Baston used both the sixth and fifth flute, while Babell wrote for solo sixth flute, two sixth flutes, and for two concert flutes.

Robert Woodcock was a recorder player of some note, as was also Baston who in 1722 played 'a new Concerto for the little flute, composed by Woodcock' at a benefit concert for Carbonelli. Babell, on the other hand, was a brilliant harpsichordist.

Recently some doubt has been cast, by Mr Brian Priestman (in *The Consort*, July 1954), on Woodcock's authorship of these concerti. Two of them are identical with some MSS at Brussels which are ascribed to Jacques Loeillet. Did Woodcock 'adopt' these works of this Loeillet? What about the other four concerti? Would not Loeillet of London have heard and possibly recognized his brother's works? Is it not equally possible that the Brussels ascriptions are mistaken, and that these concerti are in fact Woodcock's? The Brussels MSS are copies from originals at Rostock; and the true answers to these questions will not be known until those originals have been carefully examined.

The sixth flute is a delightful solo instrument to play, lighter in tone than even the descant, and not as squeaky as the sopranino. These concerti are very lightly scored, with parts for violins I and II, ripieno violins, 'cello and basso continuo, and there is so much doubling between the parts that the whole could generally be reduced to three or at the most four-part harmony. The viola, if there were one, would have played in octaves with the 'cello.

Some suites have been published which appear to have been

---

*The Sonata in A minor by Bigaglia *a Fluta di quatre e Basso* is in fact for descant recorder (=fifth flute). The composer seems to have mistakenly counted a fourth down instead of a fifth up from f!

intended originally for the fourth flute* *(flûte à quatre)*, but are now arranged for a descant recorder. Their composer was Charles Dieupart (c. 1700-1740), a Frenchman who was the harpsichordist for many of Handel's operatic performances.

While the German flute was beginning to gain favour, the recorder was at the zenith of its popularity. The popular songs of the day were hawked in the streets on song-sheets, at the foot of which was a transposition of the tune to a suitable key for the treble recorder which was called 'flute' or 'common flute'. And not only the song-sheets but collections such as *Wit Musically Embellished: being a collection of eight new English Ballads. The Words by divers eminent Hands, set to Musick with a thorough bass for the Harpsichord by Mr. John Frederick Lampe* advertised 'The Tunes all Transpos'd for the Flute'. There were four volumes of Lampe's songs, making a total of thirty-two. In Henry Carey's *The Musical Century in One Hundred English Ballads* the transposition for the flute is still, in 1740, in the compass and key of the recorder, not the transverse flute.

In 1706 was published *The First Part of the Division Flute containing a Collection of Divisions upon Several Excellent Grounds for the Flute being very Improving and Delightfull to all Lovers of that Instrument*. The art of playing divisions or variations on a many-times-repeated ground bass goes right back to Ganassi. It was revived with the development of virtuosity which was taking place in the seventeenth-century, first with Christopher Simpson's *The Division Violist* (1659) which went through many editions, and later with *The Division Violin* which Henry Playford published in 1684. Some of the grounds were used by composers of many different countries. Such was *Faronell's Ground* which was used by such masters as Corelli and Marin Marais besides finding a place in *The Division Violin* and *The Division Flute*. It is interesting to compare the versions of some of these divisions in *The Division Flute* which had already appeared twenty years earlier in John Carr's *The Delightful Companion*. Such a comparison will show that Carr indicated more 'graces' than are shown in *The Division Flute*. Compare the two versions of *An Italian Ground* (Fig. 25a):

After the appearance of Hotteterre's *Principes* in Paris in 1707 there seems to have been a gap in the production of instruction books for the recorder until a third edition of *The Compleat*

If Love's a sweet Passion. By Mr Henry Purcell.

If Love's a sweet Passion why does it torment? If a Bitter Oh tell me whence comes my Content; since I suffer with Pleasure why should I complain, or grieve at my Fate when I know 'tis in vain, yet so pleasing the Pain is. so soft is the Dart, that at once it both wounds me and tickles my Heart.

2

I press her Hand gently, look languishing down,
And by passionate Silence I make my Love known.
But Oh! how I'm blest, when so kind she does prove,
By some willing Mistake to discover her Love:
When in striving to hide, she returns all her Flame,
And our Eyes tell each other, what neither dare name.

Flute

Fig. 25

64

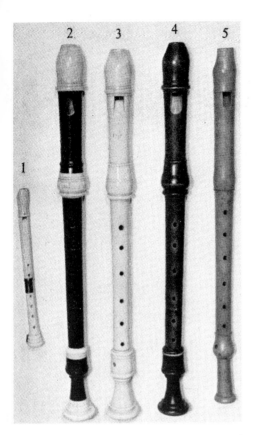

XII. RECORDERS FROM THE CARSE
COLLECTION, AT THE HORNIMAN
MUSEUM, LONDON

(1) Small ivory recorder in G, possibly
French 17th century.
(2) Treble recorder by T. Stanesby,
London, ebony with ivory mounts.
(3) Ivory Treble by J. Heitz, Berlin,
c. 1724.
(4) Treble Recorder by I. I. Schuchart,
c. 1725.
(5) Treble Recorder. Anon., of slim design.

*Photo: Horniman Museum, Forest Hill,
London.*

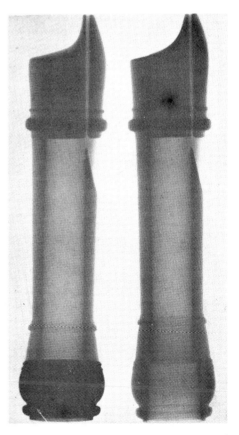

XIII. X-ray photographs of the heads of
two trebles by Bressan. Left, from the
Chester Quartet, and Right, from Eric
Halfpenny's collection.
Photo: Eric Halfpenny, Ilford, Essex.

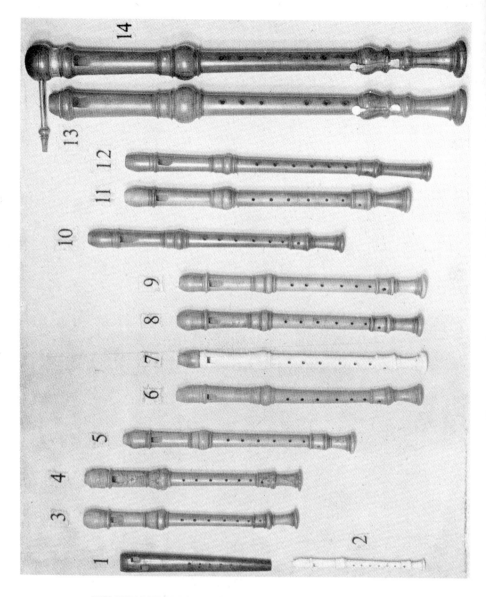

XIV. THE RECORDERS IN THE HISTORICAL MUSEUM, BASEL

(1) Flute d'accords by Christian Schlegel, Basel, first half of 18th century. (2) Ivory Sopranino by Johann Christoph Denner. (3) & (4) Boxwood trebles in G. Anon. (5) Treble F by Christian Schlegel, Basel. (6) Treble by F. Lehner. (7) Ivory treble in F. Anon. 18th century. (8) Treble F by Johann Christoph Denner. (9) Treble F by H. Schell. (10 Alto in E flat. Anon. (11) Alto in D by Rippert. (12) Alto in D. Anon. (13) Bass in G by Christian Schlegel. (14) Bass in F by Christian Schlegel.

Photo: Historical Museum, Basel.

John Carr

Division Flute

Fig. 25a

Musick-Master appeared in 1722, in which our recorder is referred to as the 'Flute'. Then in 1725 the old pattern of fingering, shakes, transposing and tunes is taken up in Walsh and Hare's publication entitled *The New Flute Master for the Year 1725 containing The most Compleat Rules and Directions for Learners on the Flute.* There is a very close parallel between this and another little book published about the same time (or perhaps a little later) by Wright and entitled *The Second Book of the Flute Master improv'd Containing the Plainest Instructions for Learners, with Variety of Easy Lessons by the Best Masters.* * Many of the tunes are identical as is also the scope of the instructions at the beginning. Both include two pages devoted to 'A Flourish or Prelude in every Key on the Flute'. 'Every key' turns out to be the following ten only: C major and minor, D minor, F major and G major, then on the second page G and A minors, B flat, E minor and D major. As compared with Hotteterre's *Principes* and *L'Art de Préluder*, the whole tendency of these and other English recorder methods was towards the amateur.

The Modern Music Master was published in 1730 or 1731 and consists of separate instruction books with tunes for amateurs who wish to learn Singing, The Flute (Recorder), The German Flute, The Hautboy, The Violin and The Harpsichord, together with a 'History of Music' and Dictionary of Musical Terms. The *Directions for Playing on the Flute* has a fine engraving of a recorder player by J. Smith as a frontispiece. *The Modern Music Master* shows the influence of Hotteterre, particularly in the German Flute section. Now there is a gap before we come to the section of four pages devoted to The Flute in William Tans'ur's *New Musical Grammar: or The Harmonical Spectator* (1746). Here we read that:

'Of *Flutes* there are many Sorts, as a *Consort-Flute:* a *Third-Flute;* a

---

*The present writer is indebted to Mr Anthony Rowland-Jones for information about this book which is in Leeds Public Library.

> *Fifth* and a *Sixth,* and *Octave-Flute;* yet all may be played by the fore-going *Rules.'*

Then, after going into the origin of the word 'flute' and 'Pan's Syringa,' we come to:

> 'Our *German-Flute* is quite different from our *Common-Flute* ... The *Bass-Flutes* are double, or quadruple its Length and Thickness; but those kind of *Instruments* are partly laid aside, and converted into *Bassoons,* &c.'

Has anyone ever seen one of these flute-bassoons? Or was Tans'ur confused by those who called the bass recorder a Basson Flûte? (cf. Weigel's *Theatrum).*

There are two and a half pages devoted to instructions for the 'Flûte-à-Bec or Common Flute' in *Apollo's Cabinet or The Muses' Delight,* which was published in Liverpool about 1754. More than a page of this is devoted to the performance of the graces: shakes, beats, double-relish, etc. and the reader is referred to other pages for Transposition.

The recorder or, as it was now called, the common flute, was still sufficiently popular to warrant a continual supply of instruction books right up to the end of the century:

c. 1754   The Compleat Tutor (for the Common Flute)
c. 1740-60   The Compleat Flute Master by John Tyther
1758-61   The Compleat Tutor for the Flute (Thomson & Son)
1779-98   Compleat Instructions for the Common Flute (Long-man & Broderip)

In 1770 Tans'ur published another book *The Elements of Music made easy* in which Chapter III is 'Of the Common Flute, or Flagelet'. The information is almost word for word the same as in his *Grammar* of 1746.

Louis Merci (or Mercy) (1690-1750), a prominent woodwind player and composer, tried, in 1732, to revive the declining popularity of the recorder in collaboration with the instrument maker T. Stanesby Junior (1692-1754). Their plan was to rationalize the notation of recorder music to agree with that of other woodwind instruments. As we know from the Concertos for the sixth flute, and music for the voice flute, the fourth flute and the fifth flute, the treble recorder in F was the standard instrument in the eighteenth century, and parts for all these instruments in D, B flat and C were transposed accordingly. On the other hand, music for the oboe, the flute and even the new clarinets in their upper register, was arranged on a system of 'six fingers D'—corresponding to the fingering of our descant recorder. Why, argued Merci, should not the recorders agree with the other woodwind? So he and Stanesby proposed to regard the recorders in C as the basis of the family, treating the treble in F and all the others as transposing instruments. The idea was, of course, the reverse of a long established system, and it never caught on.

The same idea has been tried out in our own time, by Waldemar Woehl (for many of his editions an extra *Blockflöte in F* part is provided) and by Georges Corroyez in the *Répertoire pour Flûtes douces* published by Rouart, Lerolle & Cie, Paris, 1936.

The practical disadvantages appear when it is realized that a lot of treble recorder music is played by flautists and others, and that a normal as well as the transposed part would have to be provided in the case of much solo and chamber music; and this would add quite considerably to production costs.

The age of Handel was a time of rivalries and fierce competition among composers in England. Handel himself so dominated the scene that his contemporaries are too easily overlooked. One such was Dr Johann Christoph Pepusch (1667-1752). The main points of his life were that he was a native of Berlin who settled in England in 1710 and was employed at Drury Lane in adapting operas to the needs of that theatre. He took his Doctorate at Oxford in the same year as William Croft, and was employed by the Duke of Chandos at Cannons (near Edgware—now a girls' school) and later became organist at the Charterhouse. But his chief claim to fame rests on the fact that he selected and arranged the tunes for the *Beggar's Opera*. Our interest in Pepusch lies in the fact that he left a number of works for the recorder.

First there are at least two sets of six solo sonatas. One set has been published in two editions, edited by Erna Dancker-Langer (Moeck) and F. J. Giesbert (Schott) respectively. Then there are two more edited by E. Dancker-Langer, one of which comes from a MS at Rostock, the other is to be found in two forms: in the second set of six sonatas in the British Museum, and as a duet for treble recorder and *'Fluto Basso'* at the end of some duets for two trebles also in the British Museum. In this form it is ascribed to 'Signor Papus' and was included in the music of the writer's

Practical Method. These sonatas range from No. 3 in G, which falls within the compass of a descant or tenor as well as the treble, and is constantly being murdered by youthful competitors in music festivals, to others which use the full range up to high f'''.

There is a Trio Sonata in G minor for recorder, oboe and continuo taken from a MS in the Library at Dresden; and another, for recorder, violin and continuo in C major. The latter, which is edited by Günter Hausswald, lacks any note to say where the original is to be found; so it is impossible to answer the many questions which arise when studying the score. The range of the recorder part goes below that of the treble recorder for which it is published, being from d' to c'''. It could, therefore, be played on a tenor recorder, although the frequent and prominent high Cs would be rather unsafe. It is much more likely to have been intended for the voice flute (alto in D).

The tone of the recorders is contrasted with that of violins in a Quintet in F for two treble recorders, two violins and continuo which Thurston Dart has published from a MS in his own library. There is a similar work by Gottfried Keller in which oboes can take the place of the violins, and which relies on similar antiphonal effects.

Pepusch also published a set of cantatas, including one entitled *Corydon* which has been republished in two modern editions. This attractive work is in the form of Recit., Aria, Recit., Aria. which Handel used for his Italian Cantata *Nel dolce dell' oblio*, and is for soprano voice, treble recorder and continuo.

Handel (1685-1759) himself lived at a time when the recorder and the German flute were both available to composers, and he made effective use of both. The cantata which we have just mentioned *Nel dolce dell' oblio (Pensieri notturni di Filli*—Dreams of Phyllis) must have been one of his first uses of the instrument, and is very effectively written—perhaps the atmosphere of Love called for the tone of the recorder. Love is again the theme when the recorders are employed for 'Heart, the seat of soft delight' (Fig. 26) in *Acis and Galatea*. The other two songs in *Acis* which use the recorder are of a different character. The sopranino recorder *(flauto piccolo)* imitates the birds in 'Hush, ye pretty warbling Quire' (Fig. 27), and it is for the almost humorous contrast with Polyphemus's bass voice that it is used in 'O, ruddier than the

Fig. 26

cherry'. Here the score is marked *'Flauto'* not *'Flauto piccolo'*, but Welch tells of a tradition that it used to be played on a flageo-let. The term 'flageolet' is often so inaccurately used that it might have been meant to describe a sopranino recorder. It is certainly more effective played in that way than on the ordinary treble recorder—a most amusing love song (Fig. 28).

The first publication through which Handel must have become known to the English public was his Opus 1—twelve *Solos for a German Flute a Hoboy or Violin with a Thorough Bass for the Harpsicord or Bass Violin* (Fig. 29). It comprises four for the treble recorder, marked Flauto, three for the German flute *(Traversa)*, three for the violin and the remaining two for the oboe. Although the recorder is not actually mentioned on this title page, there is no doubt that those four sonatas were intended for it, as each has the instrument's name engraved at the foot of the page. Even if this were not so, there is the evidence of the music itself which favours the different natures of the instruments. The recorder is used through its full two octaves from f' to f'''. Thurston Dart found three more sonatas in the Fitzwilliam Museum at Cambridge,

Fig. 27

the first of which, in B flat, is effective. The last movement of this is a transposition of the corresponding movement in the Violin Sonata in A. The second sonata is made up of movements found in different parts of the MS, while the third is a transposition of one of the flute *(traversa)* sonatas of Op. 1 which does not suit the nature of the recorder at all well—how can *il flauto dolce* cope with a movement marked 'furioso'?

Handel's publishers were inclined to announce his Trio Sonatas as being for two oboes or violins or flutes with continuo, in order to catch a larger public; but when all have been studied it appears that only two could be truly described as for recorder, violin and

Fig. 28

SONATA VII

Fig. 29

continuo. The one in F (Op. 2, No. 4) being an effective work and rewarding to play, the other, in C minor (Op. 2, No. 1), rather the reverse, as it lies too low for the recorder's tone to balance with the violin.

A short trio for recorders, two trebles and a bass, introduces an alto aria in *Giustino;* and in the ballet *Terpsichore* there is another trio, this time for two trebles and a violin; but it is to accompany the voice that Handel generally uses the recorders. As in the time of Purcell, the parts were usually played by the oboeists.

The effect of the recorders is enhanced by their use for special purposes only, the oboes having the more routine music to play. For example, in *Alexander's Feast, or the Power of Music. An Ode wrote in Honour of St. Cecilia by Mr. Dryden*, the audience is taken through the whole gamut of emotions. The poet starts with the wedding of Alexander and Thais—'none but the brave deserve the fair'—while Timotheus entertains the guests. Most of the time it is strings and oboes; but horns are added for the praise of Bacchus, and the trumpet for war and revenge. Then after a fiery chorus we reach the crux of the poet's argument:

> Thus, long ago,
> Ere heaving bellows learn'd to blow,
> While organs yet were mute,
> Timotheus, to his breathing flute
> And sounding lyre
> Could swell the soul to rage, or kindle soft desire.

That is where the recorders come in, and provide the prelude to a big chorus in praise of St Cecilia towards the end of the work. Just over two pages out of a hundred and sixty-six; but enough to rivet the audience's attention—a deft stroke in the dramatic tradition which we have already noted. These are the opening bars (Fig. 30):

Fig. 30

Handel never wasted a good tune, and some of those we play in the recorder sonatas and other works are also found elsewhere. The recorder Sonata in F turns up as an organ concerto, while the fugue from the C major sonata is found again in the Overture to *Scipio,* and the little Minuet in *Terpsichore* is transposed to B flat to fit into a trio sonata. Instances such as these could be multiplied. Among the composers who worked successfully under the Handelian shadow was Dr Thomas Augustine Arne (1710-1778). In his operas he generally scored for traversi; but some of his best-known works are his settings of Shakespeare's songs, including 'Under the Greenwood tree'; and there we find him making appropriate use of the sopranino recorder. The same little instrument is used in the cantata *The Morning,* and it appears again in *The Wood Nymph.*

From Handel in England let us turn to his old friend in Hamburg, Johann Mattheson (1684-1764), with whom he fought the famous duel. Mattheson was secretary to the British Ambassador, a man of great influence and many talents: writer, composer, and opera singer. He appreciated the recorder and, unlike many musicians today, acknowledged that it was the only woodwind instrument that could be played in tune in any key. One can compare his assessment of the recorder and the flute from his *Neueröffnete Orchester* (1713). He speaks thus of the recorder:
'Ob nun gleich eine solche Flûte douce das allerleichteste Instrument ist und scheinet, so fatiguiret es doch den Spieler so wol als den Zuhörer, wenn es sich zu lange hören läszt. Denn dem ersten kostet eine Flûte vielmehr Wind als ein Basson, Hautbois, oder Traversière, und der andere kan ihrer, wegen der sanfften und kriechenden Eigenschaft leicht müde und überdrüszig werden.'*
and of the transverse flute, in a parallel passage:
'. . . ist das Instrument, welches, verständigen Ausspruch nach, einer moderirten Menschen Stimme (nicht aber eines bölckenden Küsters seiner) am allernähesten kommen will, und folglich, wenn es mit Jugement gespielet wird, hoch zu estimiren ist.†

---

*Though the flute douce is and appears to be the easiest of all, it nevertheless tires player and hearer alike if played for too long. Because the former needs so much more breath for the recorder than for a bassoon, oboe or transverse flute, and because the latter can easily tire of its soft and insidious quality.

†. . . is the instrument which, according to a common saying, tries to come closest to the modulation of the human voice (but not to that of a bleating cantor), and which therefore should be highly appreciated if played with good judgement.

But, for recorder players, the chief interest, as in the case of Handel, lies in Mattheson's Opus 1, *XII Sonates à 2 et 3 flutes sans bass,* which were published in 1708 by Roger of Amsterdam. The first two and last two are duets for two trebles, while the middle eight are for three trebles. Every player will have his favourites, but all are well written, and give the impression that Mattheson might have played the recorder as a boy (Fig. 31). Mattheson's other compositions, such as the solo sonatas with continuo, are for the traversa.

Fig. 31

The sonatas for three trebles by Mattheson stand almost alone, but Giesbert has edited two sonatas (also Op. 1), for the same combination by Johann Scherer.

Many of the German 'Kapellmeister' composers at this time wrote for recorders, but we must be content with mentioning three: Pez, Heinichen and Graupner.

Johann Christoph Pez (1664-1716) was a native of Munich who worked there, also at Liège, Bonn and finally at the court at Stuttgart. He is best known to recorder players from the beautiful *Pastorale* which is the first movement of his *Concerto Pastorale* for two treble recorders, strings and continuo. The other movements are two *Arias,* an *Aria: Pastorale* which returns to the mood of the first movement, a *Minuet,* an extended Chaconne with a final *Presto.* Then there are pieces for recorders with two and with three viole d'amore, viola and bass, consisting of an *Overture* followed by a number of *Arias* and dance movements. And lastly trios for two trebles and continuo, and an attractive *Adagio* and *Presto* for recorder and continuo.

Heinichen and Graupner were fellow students, Johann David Heinichen (1683-1729) wrote a brilliant Concerto for four treble recorders, strings and continuo. The disposition of the parts is unusual, being for *Flauto concertato, Flauti ripieni* I, II and III, and the normal strings. There are four movements: *Allegro, Pastorell, Adagio* (solo recorder and continuo), and *Allegro assai,* of which the *Pastorell* offers the most beautiful effect of a melody over long sustained notes. There is another *Concerto,* in G, for recorder, two violins and continuo, a combination used by Scarlatti and others.

Christoph Graupner (1683-1760) had a distinct flair for instrumentation; as can be heard in his Concerto for recorder and strings, the slow movement of which is a most beautiful solo with pizzicato accompaniment. His suites for three *Chalumeaux* (proto-clarinets) though not original music for recorder, provide interesting trio material for two trebles and tenor. They are in the form of Overture + dances, which is found at its best in Bach's B minor Flute Suite. This same form is to be found in the *Parties sur les Fleut dous à 3*—an original trio for treble, tenor and bass recorders, the MS of which is in the Library at Wolfenbüttel. The clue to the identity of the author lies in the initials J. C. F. on the title page (Fig. 31a). Those are the initials of Johann Christoph Faber, a composer who flourished about 1730, and the piece must be unique as an example of chamber music for treble, meane and bass in this time. Its attractive simplicity has led to the appearance of more than one edition of the original, as well as arrangements for des-

Fig. 31a

cant, treble and tenor.

Leaving the lesser German composers of the first half of the eighteenth-century, the great Johann Sebastian Bach (1685-1750) next demands attention. Bach's use of the recorder is so varied and so subtle, and he demands such skill from his players, that a whole volume could be written on the subject. But let us first clear away certain doubts. His solo sonatas, the sonatas for flute and harpsichord, the trio sonatas, the B minor Suite and the two concerti for flute, violin and harpsichord (Brandenburg V, and in A minor) are all for traversa. So there are none of the smaller chamber works for recorder, and we have to begin with the two Brandenburg Concerti, Nos. II and IV, and the F major version of No. IV which is classed with the harpsichord concerti.

In Brandenburg II the soloists are flute (= treble recorder), oboe, trumpet and violin; and the chief headache is the trumpet part—how it should be performed and balanced. The problem disappears in the slow movement, but is with us again for the finale. Since the art of *Clarino* playing was lost with the advent of valves, there have been many attempted solutions—playing the part an octave lower, or an octave lower in parts, giving some phrases to the flute, playing the part on a saxophone or on a clarinet—besides trying to play it as Bach wrote it! But these are not the recorder player's problems provided the trumpet is not allowed to dominate.

Another set of problems surround Brandenburg IV in G major for solo violin and two *Flauti d'Echo*. The writer used to think that the many existing baroque trebles in G might have been intended for these parts and that *Flauto d'Echo* might have been the name for such an instrument. Then there was the possibility that ordinary trebles were intended, as has been shown convincingly by the performances of Carl Dolmetsch and others. A further possibility has been pleaded by Thurston Dart, with many plausible arguments; and that is that *Flauto d'Echo* was not a recorder at all but a flageolet, and that the part should sound an octave higher than written. His argument falls a little when he has to admit that the compass of the flageolet was not quite equal to it, but he does not reach the stage of suggesting sopranino recorders, which would be just as probable.*

*Sopraninos have been tried (12 August 1961), but unconvincingly.

In the F major harpsichord version there is not the same problem as the parts are clearly *Flûte à bec* and fit perfectly both in range and balance.

All that recorder players miss in solo music is made up in the Church Cantatas which include some of the most wonderful music; and there is one place in the *St Matthew* Passion where the recorders are called for to replace the traversi. That is the *Recitative and Chorus* No. 25 *O Schmerz! hier zittert das gequälte Herz* which is scored for two recorders, two oboi da caccia and continuo, and where we contemplate the Man of Sorrows immediately after the 'Agony in the Garden'.

We shall take the Cantatas themselves in chronological order in order to explain some of the problems of their performance. As these works were for use in particular churches, the different pitches of their respective organs had to be taken into account, and this often meant that the wind parts had to be transposed— sometimes as much as a minor third. Bach never scored for the transverse flute until after 1716, the year in which he visited Dresden in order to hear the operatic performances there. It was at Dresden that Pierre Gabriel Buffardin was principal flute *(traversa)* in the Court orchestra. He was a Frenchman who brought the improvements of Hotteterre to Germany, and who greatly impressed Quantz, who also visited Dresden in 1716. Buffardin retained his Court appointment until 1730 and died about 1739.

The first surviving Cantata to include recorder parts is No. 71 *Gott ist mein König* (1708), a festival work in praise of the Kaiser Joseph, and performed in the Marienkirche at Mühlhausen where the recorders were evidently in tune with the organ.

Cantata 106, the *Actus tragicus: Gottes Zeit* has some wonderful music for the recorders which, with two viole da gamba and the continuo, provide the whole accompaniment. The fact that the recorder parts are transposed a tone higher than the organ part points to performance in the Stadtkirche at Weimar, and not the Ducal Palace which would have necessitated a minor third's difference. The Cantata was probably composed for a service commemorating Philipp Grossgebauer, Rector of Weimar until 1711. Here is the old association of the recorders with the solemn moment of death. The opening *Sonatina* is a beautiful instrumental piece in which the two recorder parts are closely woven above the viols and bass (Fig. 32).

Fig. 32

The next, No. 142, was composed some time between 1712 and 1714 and is the Christmas Cantata *Uns ist ein Kind geboren*. The opening *Concerto* is complete in itself and is scored for two recorders, two oboes and strings; and there is the aria *Jesu, Dir sei Preis* for mezzo-soprano with two recorders and continuo, which is very popular with amateur groups.

Cantata 18 was composed in 1714—*Gleichwie Regen und Schnee*. The opening *Sinfonia* provides an interesting exercise in 'clef transposition', as the flutes play in octaves with the violas for most of the time. The violas are written in G minor, while the recorders, with the notes in the same positions on the staff, are reading in A minor with the French violin clef. This means that the recorders were either tenors in B flat (or possibly 'fourth flutes') or again, it may have just been a normal whole-tone transposition.

The scoring itself is unusual, being for two recorders, four violas, bassoon, violoncello and continuo.

We have already noted that the•organ at the Ducal Palace at Weimar was at the high *Cornett-Ton* necessitating a minor third transposition in order that *Kammer-Ton* wind instruments could agree. This helps to prove that *Himmelskönig, sei willkommen,* No. 182, belongs to the years 1714-15, for here the recorder parts are in B flat and the organ, etc. in G. Here there is an opening *Sonata* for *Flauto concertato, Violino concertato* and strings.

Again we have the minor third transposition in the case of Cantata 161, *Komm, du süsse Todesstunde* (1715). This is another funeral cantata, one in which the hour of death strikes realistically like a clock.

Tritt auf die Glaubensbahn (No. 152, 1715) is unique in its instrumentation, being for two solo voices, a high soprano and a bass of wide range, recorder, oboe, viola d'amore, viola da gamba and continuo. The introduction is a beautiful *Adagio and Fugue* for the instruments, and there is the aria, *Stein, der über alle Schätze,* with obbligati for recorder and viola d'amore, in which the soprano sings of Christ the Corner-stone. The minor third transposition puts this rather high for any but a true soprano.

The most famous of arias with recorders obbligati is *Schafe können sicher weiden,* known familiarly as 'Sheep'. This comes from a secular cantata, and the Aria is sung by Pales the god of shepherds. It was written to celebrate the birthday in 1716 of the Duke Christian of Sax-Weissenfels. Having nothing to do with the church the continuo could be played on a harpsichord and there were no transposition problems. The title of the Cantata was *Was mir behagt, ist nur die muntre Jagd.* Here was clearly a pastoral song in a cantata in honour of a leading huntsman.

The last Cantata of the Weimar period to use recorders was No. 189, *Meine Seele rühmt und preist* (1715-18), which contains two arias accompanied by recorder, oboe and continuo. This Cantata was not transposed for the flutes as were most of the others of this period, and critics say that it and No. 142 (also untransposed) are of doubtful authenticity.

At Köthen Bach did not have the same opportunities for cantatas in the church, but this was the period when he composed the Brandenburg Concertos. Lastly we have the Leipzig period, and the next Cantata to have recorder parts is reminiscent of *Gott ist mein König,* the Mühlhausen *Ratswahlkantate* of 1708. This Leipzig *Ratswahlkantate* is No. 119 *Preise, Jerusalem, den Herrn* (1723). Apart from an alto aria *Die Obrigkeit ist Gottes Gabe* with two recorders and continuo, the recorders are treated as tutti instruments; and the same is true of No. 65 *Sie werden aus Saba alle kommen* (1724). Then we come to one of the most beautiful arias of all: *Jesus schläft, was soll ich hoffen,* for alto, from the Cantata of the same title (No. 81, 1724).

The Cantata *Schauet doch und sehet* (No. 46, 1727) contains the alto aria *Doch Jesus will* with the unusual accompaniment of two recorders and oboe da caccia (with two players in unison) without the customary continuo. The recorders join in other movements including the Choral which uses the same material as the *Qui tollis* of the Mass in B minor (where flutes play the recorder parts and the key is different).

The *St Matthew* Passion belongs to 1729, and the F major setting of Brandenburg IV was probably made about this time; then in 1731/32 we come to the first of the cantatas to use three recorders. This is *Es ist nicht Gesundes* (No. 25), and in the aria *Öffne meine schlechten Liedern* the first recorder reaches the high F sharp and G. We have three recorders again in the pastoral atmosphere of *Er rufet seinen Schafen* (No. 175, 1735).

In the *St Matthew* Passion we have the recorders in only one number out of seventy-eight and the traversi in thirty-six, and the *flûte-à-bec* is not marked for that number in all scores. But in the *Easter Oratorio* there can be no doubt that the recorders are used in the tenor aria *Sanfte soll mein Todeskummer* for the beautiful undulating accompaniment, while the *traversa* also has its own obbligato.

About 1740 (some authorities give 1732 as the date) Bach wrote Cantata 39, *Brich dem Hungrigen dein Brot.* The occasion was a special one. The Archbishop of Salzburg had turned thousands of Protestants from his domain, and they came as refugees to Leipzig, where the citizens fed, clothed and gave them shelter, and on the Sunday a special service with this Cantata. The soprano aria, *Höchster, was ich habe,* requires an obbligato for two recorders in unison.

Tenderness is the quality one finds in so many of Bach's recorder

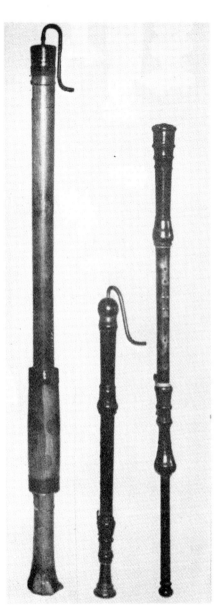

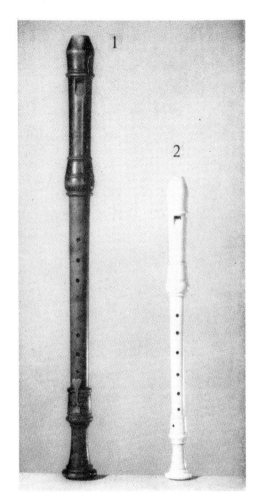

XVI. Tenor recorder in B flat by
Stanesby Junior with ivory treble
(anon) from Dr Walter Bergmann's
collection. The key on the tenor is
not original.

XV. Basses from the Institute of
Theatre, Music and Cinematography,
Leningrad. Great Bass 165 cm long
with maker's mark below the lip.
Bass, 90 cm long, by I. C. Denner,
covered with black lacquer. Bass by
T. Boekhout with supporting post,
of boxwood stained dark reddish-
brown.

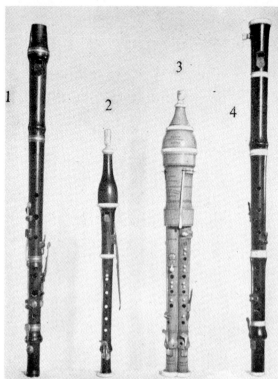

XVII. THE DECLINE AND FALL OF THE RECORDER

(1) This is stamped with a crown and 'Improved patent voice flute, London'. (2) An English flageolet by Bainbridge. The long key at the side provides 'semitones' by raising the pitch of the whole instrument. (3) A double flageolet by Simpson after Bainbridge's patent. (4) A fipple-flute by Bainbridge, 'New Patent', blown from the side to look like a transverse flute. *From the writer's collection.*

XVIII. Machine for drilling all holes in a descant recorder at the same time.

Photo: W. Schreiber & Söhne

XIX. A corner of a recorder maker's workshop in Germany.

Photo:
W. Schreiber & Söhne

parts. It is found again in Cantata 13, *Meine Seufzer, meine Tränen* (about 1740), in which the recorders are again joined by the oboi da caccia; and the same can be said of Cantata 180, *Schmücke dich, o liebe Seele* (1740-44).

Three recorders and continuo accompany the soprano in a recitative in the Cantata, *Das neugeborne Kindelein,* for the Sunday after Christmas (No. 122, 1740-44). To the same period belongs *Herr Jesu Christ, wahr'r Mensch und Gott* (No. 127, 1740-44) where the scoring is for two recorders, two oboes and strings, as in many others such as Nos. 39 and 142.

All these recorder parts, with the possible exception of Cantata 18, are for treble. There remain two other cantatas where Bach calls for a higher instrument. In Cantata 103, *Ihr werdet weinen und heulen* (1735) there is a part for a *Flauto Piccolo* in the opening chorus. The piccolo part is in D minor, and this, if played on a Sixth Flute, would sound in B minor which is the key of the piece. The other is in Cantata 96, *Herr Christ, der ein'ge Gottes Sohn* (1740) where the sopranino plays *col violino piccolo.*

These cantatas of Bach are the richest store for the recorder player to explore, and every performance enhances one's love for their music.

To the musical world of the eighteenth century Bach was only second best. Telemann came first—the most famous, the most skilled, and the most prolific. Then came the nineteenth-century revival of Bach's music, and Telemann became no more than a name in a dictionary, unnoticed by the history books, and sneered at—'he wrote so much so quickly, that none of it can be any good'. Then, in the 1930s, recorder players looked in the libraries of Europe and began to discover Telemann: we played the F major Sonata from *Der Getreue Musikmeister,* and before long the rest of the world began to discover Telemann. Never before has there been a greater change in the assessment of a great composer than has happened in the case of Telemann; and recorder players were, in the first instance, responsible for it.

Georg Philipp Telemann was born in 1681, at Magdeburg. He was musically self-taught, but became a master of his art through the study of the works of others, including Lully. After spending part of his youth at Hildesheim he entered the University of Leipzig in 1700, and while studying there, became, in 1704, organist at the Neukirche. At this time he formed a musical society, called a 'Collegium Musicum', among the students.

After holding the office of Kapellmeister (1708) at Eisenach (among other important positions both there and at Frankfurt) he was appointed, in 1721, cantor at the Johanneum, and musical director of the chief church in Hamburg, posts which he held until he died in 1767. He travelled widely, making frequent visits to Berlin and other musical centres; and his later works show marked traces of French influences, following a long stay there in 1737, and Polish styles after a visit to that country.

Starting with Telemann's duets there are two from his publication *Der getreue Musikmeister:* one in B flat for two trebles and the other in the same key for treble recorder and violin. This

Fig. 33

second sonata is also published in a version for traversa and violin in G. This is explained by the system of clef transposition which was used in those days. Write out your music in G with the ordinary treble clef for the flute: if you want a more comfortable key for the range of the treble recorder, put the French violin clef and two flats at the beginning and you can play the same notes in B flat. Take the same notes with alto clef and three sharps, and you have a piece for viols! Many of Telemann's duets for two German flutes have now been reprinted in transposed editions for recorders both in England and in Germany. Some are very welcome additions to the recorder's repertory, but others do not fit so comfortably.

Of Telemann's sonatas for treble recorder and continuo, eight are now available: two from the *Essercizii Musici,* in D minor and C, four from *Der getreue Musikmeister,* in F, C, F minor and C. Of these, that in F minor is a bassoon sonata which by exchanging the French violin clef for the bass clef, can be played on the recorder. One of those in C is in canon and appears in B flat as a viola sonata, but can also be played as a duet for viol and recorder or as a recorder sonata. Then there is a second F minor sonata. The eighth has been included in Carl Dolmetsch's *School Recorder Book III.*

On the border line between duos and trios there is the Sonata in B flat for recorder and harpsichord, with a separate continuo part for a viola da gamba or a second harpsichord!

Among the trios are the many trio sonatas in which the recorder and harpsichord are joined by a second recorder, a violin, an oboe or a viola da gamba, and among these we find some of Telemann's most beautiful and effective music. For two trebles and continuo there is the Sonata in F, another in C (in which many of the movements portray the characters of ladies of antiquity: Xanthippe, Corinna, Dido, etc.) and a third in G minor. Many of the violin and oboe trios can be adapted for two recorders where the second part keeps within a reasonable compass. Of those published for recorder, violin and continuo, many were intended by their composer to have the second part played on a treble viol rather than a violin, and many of these would fit a second recorder; on the other hand some others have true violin parts, for which other instruments cannot substitute. One in which the violin is in contrast to the recorder is in A minor with a charming Minuet and unaccompanied trio in A major at the end. On the other hand there is one in C in which the two parts are identical since they are in canon throughout, but have a freshness which prevents the work from smelling of the lamp. A brilliant *Sonata* a 3 has been found at Brussels. This is in D minor, and opens with a dialogue between the two treble instruments. There is a second A in minor, and one in F minor. In this key the violin loses some of its open-string brilliance and matches the recorder tone more closely. Telemann, however, achieves an admirable balance by using the higher register of the recorder when he wants it to seem the stronger instrument.

Of the Trio Sonatas in which another instrument, such as a tenor recorder, can substitute for the violin, there are at least four: two in F major, G minor and D minor respectively.

For treble recorder, oboe and continuo there are sonatas in F major, E, A and C minors of which the last is the writer's favourite. There is a trio (or 'Concerto') for recorder, horn and continuo and finally a Trio in F for recorder, viola da gamba and continuo with interesting syncopations in the opening theme and a brilliant and difficult finale.

The quartets present some interesting combinations under various titles. There are two for recorder, oboe, violin and continuo, one a 'Concerto a 4' in A minor; the other available in two versions, in F and G respectively, has a brilliant *concertato* violin part the two wind instruments work together more smoothly. There is a Quadro for recorder, violin, viola and continuo and a quartet for recorder (or bassoon), two transverse flutes and continuo. In this the recorder has the more important part.

The next step is to the solo concerti: the Suite in A minor for treble recorder and string orchestra, and the Konzertsuite in F major (published) for the same instrumentation. The latter was originally a tone lower, in E flat, for a *Flute pastorelle,* which Adolf Hoffmann, who has edited the work, takes to be an E flat alto recorder—such instruments existed: there is one at Chester. However that may be, Carl Dolmetsch has played the F major version on a descant recorder, and this gives it a far more brilliant concerto effect than would be possible on a treble. So it seems more likely that *Flute pastorelle* was another name for the B flat descant or 'fourth flute', an opinion which is confirmed by Dr Bergmann. A *Concerto di Camera* in G minor is published as *Eine Kammermusik* and uses the same orchestra without violas as the Concerti of Woodcock, Heinichen and Scarlatti. Then we come to the great Concerto in F which is for recorder and the normal string orchestra and which exploits the highest notes of the treble recorder, up to c''''. We must remember that the fingerings of these notes (except the high c) were well known as they were given in Majer's *Museum Musicum.* There is also a Concerto in C.

Lastly we come to the double concertos and the *Concerti Grossi.* There are concertos in B flat and A minor for two trebles and strings, one for recorder and flute in E minor and one for recorder and viola da gamba in A minor. There are three *concerti grossi* for two recorders, two oboes and strings, in B flat, A minor and F respectively, and one for two recorders, two flutes, two oboes and strings.

Amongst Telemann's enormous output there are the seventy-two cantatas of his *Harmonische Gottesdienst.* Each of these consists of *recit, aria, recit, aria,* the arias having instrumental obbligati in which Telemann rings the changes between violin, oboe, recorder and flute—a cantata for each Sunday and festival of the Christian year.

The novice may be appalled at the difficulty of much of

Telemann's music, but will find some comfort in the *Wedding Divertissement* which can be played on a descant recorder with piano accompaniment, and then dip into the volume of *Die Kleine Kammermusik* which consists of six Partitas for violin, flute or oboe; but which can be played very well on a descant recorder.

Johann Joachim Quantz (1697-1773) was a musician of great influence in the eighteenth century, both through his book *Versuch einer Anweisung die* Flûte Traversière *zu spielen*, and through his position as Frederick the Great's flute teacher and court composer at Potsdam. As a flautist he ignored the recorder in his book—he did not, like Hotteterre, include a section for it; but this did not prevent him from including the recorder with the flute in a charming Trio Sonata in C, with the violin in another in the same key, and with the viola d'amore in yet another in F.

We have already noted three chamber works in which the recorder and flute combine: Telemann's Concerto for recorder, flute and strings, his Quartet for recorder, two flutes and continuo, and Quantz's Trio Sonata. But we must not forget the Quartet for two recorders and one flute with continuo by Johann Friedrich Fasch (1688-1758) who was court composer at Zerbst. Fasch also composed an interesting *Canon Sonata a 3; Flûte à bec, Fagotto e Cembalo* in F major, in which the bassoon plays in canon, an octave and a fourth below the recorder.

While the English had their Most Pleasant, Genteel, and Delightful Companions and their Compleat and Modern Musick-Masters, and while the French studied Hotteterre, the Germans had Majer's *Museum Musicum* (1732 and 1741) and Eisel's *Musikus Autodidaktos* (1738) which has a section on the *Fleute douce*. The book which we refer to simply as Majer was *Museum Musicum Theoretico Practicum, das ist Neu-eröffneter Theoretisch- und Practischer Music-Saal. . . . . .von Joseph Friederich Bernhard Caspar Majer*. This book is of importance, as it is one of the few since Ganassi to explore the very high notes above g'''. In addition to giving a fingering for the recorder's problem note, the high F sharp, he gives fingerings for G sharp, A, B flat and B natural. Strangely he omits the high C which Telemann uses in both the Sonata in F from *Der getreue Musik-meister* and the Concerto in F. Majer's *Flöthen* are, like Agricola's about two hundred years earlier, given four names for only three sizes: the Discant is in f', the Alt—or Tenor-*Flöthe* in c' and the bass in f.

Writing in 1784, C.F.D. Schubart said of the recorder: 'This instrument has almost gone out of use owing to its too-quiet tone and limited compass'. *(Ideen zu einer Aesthetik der Tonkunst,* p. 209).

Although the flute went ahead in professional circles the recorder was no doubt still used among amateurs in the smaller towns, and something very much like a recorder, but called a csakan, was sufficiently popular, about 1830, for B. Schotts Söhne of Mainz to bring out a *Csakan-Schule.* Here the csakan is identified with the flute douce, and, according to the table of

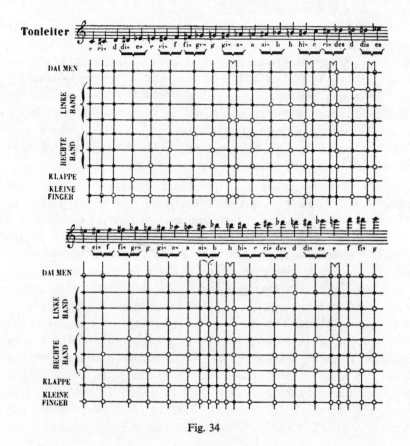

Fig. 34

fingerings, had a range of two octaves and a fifth (c' to g'''). The table also shows that it had the seven finger-holes and thumb hole of the recorder with the addition of a D sharp key. The csakan was evidently treated as a transposing instrument, its actual pitch being from a flat to e''' flat (so it says in the book— probably an octave higher in fact). The fingering and instructions are followed by ten little duets for two csakans.

There is also the possibility that some of Haydn's little trios for flute and strings were published for those who still played the recorder as well as those who had the newer flutes, and that the flute parts of many of his symphonies were for traversière or à bec.

*   *   *

With the growth of opera and vocal music and the rapid development of music for the violin family, a great tide of Italian music surged through Europe in the seventeenth and eighteenth centuries, only to be checked by the German and later Viennese instrumental schools. Italy exported many composers and players to England, among them Barsanti, Bononcini and Sammartini. From Francesco Barsanti (1690-1770?) we have some very fine recorder sonatas. He came here with Geminiani in 1714 and became oboeist at the Italian Opera. Later he married a Scots girl and lived in Scotland. He returned to London in 1750 where he played the viola in theatre orchestras. In his old age he was supported by his daughter who was a talented singer and actress, and who married one of the leaders of the Dublin theatre. Giovanni Battista Bononcini (c. 1660-1750) was famous as Handel's rival in the operatic field, but also composed some chamber music. Among his works for the recorder are a *Divertimento da Camera* for recorder and continuo and some trio sonatas. There were two brothers Sammartini, and of them Gioseffo (also known as Guiseppe) Sammartini or St Martino became known as the 'London Sammartini'. He was born at Milan about 1693 and came to England as Chamber Musician, playing the oboe, to the Prince of Wales. It is not known for certain when he died—some say 1740, others 1770. His contribution to the recorder's repertory was a set of twelve Trio Sonatas for two treble recorders and continuo, which are gay and full of original touches; and a brilliant Concerto in F for descant recorder and string orchestra.

There are recorder sonatas (with continuo) by Benedetto Marcello 1686-1739) and by the violinist Francesco Maria Veracini (1690-1768); but the composers who did most to keep instrumental music alive in Italy were Alessandro Scarlatti (1659-1725) and Antonio Vivaldi (1678-1741).

Scarlatti's Sonata for three treble recorders and continuo is a most attractive work in three movements: the first is a smooth-flowing mingling of sounds, the second light and based on a rising hexachord, and finally a Minuet of charming simplicity. Then there are a number of concertos: a *Sonata* for recorder, two violins and bass, a *Sinfonia,* No. 1, in F for two recorders and strings, *Sinfonia* No. 4, in E minor, for recorder, oboe and strings and No. 5 in D minor for two recorders and strings.

One of the most beautiful Trios involving the recorder must surely be that by Vivaldi, for recorder, oboe and continuo in G minor. It is in three movements: *Allegro ma cantabile, Largo* and *Allegro non molto.* Much further research is needed to decide which works, from the quantity of Vivaldi's instrumental music being published by Ricordi, are rightly for the transverse-flute, and which really belong to the recorder. Malipiero's edition gives no help in differentiating between the two instruments. The Concerto in C major (F. VI No. 4) for *ottavino*, strings and cembalo seems to point to the sopranino. It is known that the six concertos of his Op. 10 were originally for recorder, but published by Vivaldi as for the traversa when that instrument became so much more popular. But the rest await a true assessment.

There never was a second *Fontegara*, and until recently it would seem that musicians in Italy thought only of opera, singing and strings.

Before the recorder finally disappeared from the scene, there were some interesting uses of the instrument. In opera Paisiello gave it the obbligato to a charming air in his *Barber of Seville* (popular before Rossini's); and the writer is convinced that the famous flute solo in Gluck's *Orfeo* was intended for the recorder and not the *traversa*, on the internal evidence of the music. In spite of Berlioz's ecstatic statements about the 'veiled F natural'of the flute, the piece fits the recorder better; and, in this use of the instrument, Gluck would have been following the old tradition of using the recorder for 'other-worldly' occasions.

K. P. E. Bach wrote an interesting trio for recorder, viola and continuo. Different MSS give different instrumentations for this work, but in the published edition the recorder is a bass recorder, an unique use of the instrument. In these days of Tertis violas, the problems of balance weigh heavily against an effective performance; but if the viola player treats the music gently it can be achieved. Other 'late' works are the trio sonatas of Schultz (1733-1813) for two treble recorders and continuo.

5

THE DESIGN OF RECORDERS
AND RECORDER MAKERS

Since the sixteenth century there have been many changes in the design of recorders, some so slight as to pass unnoticed except by the expert, others marking important changes in construction and playing technique.

The sixteenth century is marked by simplicity of design. Take first the tenors—made of one piece of wood, with sometimes only a very slight 'beak for a mouthpiece, and this often on the under side so that the opening and lip are on the same side as the thumb hole. Even when this opening and lip are on the top, in line with the finger holes, the beak is generally small. Then a gentle narrowing follows the line of the inner bore most of the way down before gently flaring out to provide the thickness necessary to prevent damage to the lower end. Being of one piece the *neuf trous* principle is followed. For examples of such instruments see Praetorius's woodcut, and Plate IX No. 1 and Plate VII. In the case of some smaller instruments the holes are all placed in line; Plate VIII No. 2 and Plate XII No. 1.

Coming next to the larger instruments, anything longer than about 2 ft. probably needs a key for the lowest note. This is

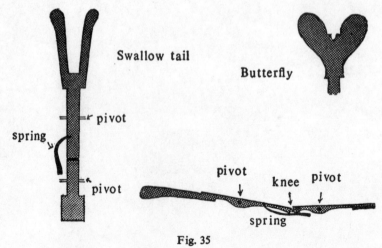

Fig. 35

centrally placed and of simple design, with a 'butterfly' or 'swallow tail' touch. As this is an open-standing key it needs only a light spring to keep it open except when pressed down by the player, and to return it to the open position afterwards. This can function as shown by Mersenne by pressing down the 'knee'. Such a key would be protected by a fontanelle or barrel-shaped cover, made of wood, perforated, and fitted with metal rings at top and bottom for strength. The perforations provide opportunities for various 'rose' designs, and the metal rings were often engraved (see Burney's description page 24). This fontanelle would have provided a bulge, equal or larger in diameter than the head of the instrument, at what would otherwise be its slimmest point. So, to give a more finished design, such recorders are given a more definite foot. (Plates V, VII and XV).

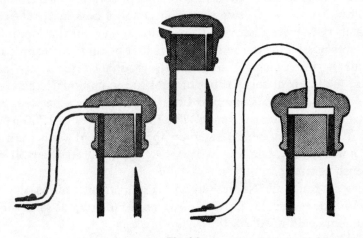

Fig. 36

Instruments of the large tenor or basset range will have to be blown from the back (or provided with a crook to the same purpose). This is generally arranged by providing a mouthpiece cap with a slot at the rear, or two or more holes side by side in place of the slot. With the larger basses the problems are similar but magnified. They are now too large for direct blowing, and a crook is essential. In the earlier recorders this generally enters the top.

The inner bore of the renaissance recorders is wide in proportion to the length, mainly because the taper is not as acute as is the case with the later instruments. This, of course, influences the tone quality, favouring the fundamentals and giving the solemn sound noticed by early writers. The makers somehow managed to provide these instruments with finger holes sufficiently close together to be manageable—no mean feat considering the size of some of them.

Praetorius was the first to mention the making of recorders with separate head joints so that they could be tuned together.

Although recorders in C and F were well established in the second half of the seventeenth century and the Hotteterres had introduced their changes, instruments of older pattern were still being made about the year 1700, for that is the date ascribed to the fine set of recorders by Hieronymus Franziskus Kynsker which can be seen in the German National Museum at Nürnberg.

Plate VII shows the seven instruments of this set. Two descants in D, two trebles in G, two tenors in D and a bass in G. The case in which they were discovered showed that an eighth, a sopranino in G, was missing from the set, and made it possible to reconstruct the missing instrument. The case itself was shaped like a very large syrinx, made up of seven tubes of sizes to accommodate the seven larger recorders. The sopranino fitted into the space between the two trebles and the two tenors. The museum gives c. 1700 as the date of these instruments, but they appear to be of a much earlier type and Victor Mahillon, writing in 1909, placed them in the sixteenth century:

'Le jeu de flûtes de Nuremberg est certainement unique et nous offre un document des plus précieux pour l'histoire de la musique instrumentale au XVI° siècle . . . '

and about the case:

' . . . On trouve la représentation d'un étui semblable dans les gravures de J. Amman, né à Zurich en 1539, mort en 1591 à Nuremberg.'

The two descants have the lowest hole in line—there is no difficulty for the little finger of either hand to stretch (the same feature can be seen in the ivory descant from Munich (Plate VIII No. 2), but the others follow the pattern of the *flûtes à neuf trous*. The design of the head joints, which are separate (Praetorius pattern) for tuning, is attractive and unusual. The bass has no crook, being blown from the back.

Occasionally one finds a recorder of an eccentric design. For instance, there are three recorders known to the writer, of a most unusual columnar shape. In Brussels there is the treble in G (at a very flat pitch), while in Paris there are the corresponding tenor in C and bass in F. In this sketch of the bass (Fig. 37) the shaded parts are of brass, and the instrument stands like a pillar about 99 cm high. The crook is probably not original, but there would have to be some kind of mouthpiece at the back. The brass fitting at the top covers the opening and lip. The instrument is made on 'neuf trous' principles, and the little brass doors below the crook (there are two—one each side) open to reveal two thumb holes. Below that, there is a brass cover to hide the opening at the end of the tube, and on the left in the sketch are the six finger holes and the two keys (each with swallow-tail touch).

The tenor and treble are both blown through a little slot at the back of the 'capital' but are otherwise similar, the tenor being 70 cm and the treble 51 cm high. These instruments probably belong to the sixteenth century, and are stamped with trefoil maker's marks similar to that found on Rauch von Schrattenbach's instruments.

The changes that were made in the design of recorders in the latter half of the seventeenth century stemmed from the fuller adoption of the idea of making the instrument in separate jointed sections. This gave scope for the turner's skill. Gone was the simple line of the sixteenth-century tenors. The new joints needed extra strength from the thickening of the material at these places. The thickness was provided, but smoothed into the general line of the instrument. In the case of the more precious recorders ivory was used, sometimes to tip the joints and mouthpiece, at others for the whole instrument.

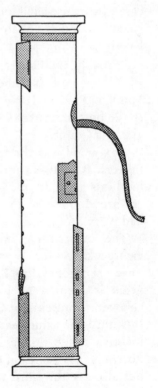

Fig. 37

The use of ivory invited the craftsman to decorate his work either by carving, as in the case of the sixth flutes by Stanesby Junior (in the writer's possession Plate IX No. 3) and W. Beukers (Dayton Miller Collection No. 1257, Plate XI); or by engraving as in the two anonymous instruments, a treble and sopranino, in the Dayton Miller collection (Nos. 945 and 1259, Plate XI). The simple design in ivory is seen in the sixth flute by T. Stanesby (Miller 1214), shown in the same plate.

The quality of tone one gets with these ivory recorders is generally less mellow than that of the wooden instruments, but they are, nevertheless, musical instruments in the fullest sense—not *stromenti non usati*. The same cannot always be said of the recorders made of tortoise-shell and gold pique (or rather covered with it), as too often the wood base has shrunk, leaving the outside case of tortoise-shell loose. Such instruments are to be found at The Hague, London (Victoria and Albert—said to have belonged to Rossini), Vienna and in other museums.

Probably the largest ivory recorder is the bass in F, 87 cm long, by Denner of Nürnberg, in the Bavarian National Museum at Munich (Plate VIII No. 1). The beauty of this instrument is rather spoilt by the written inscription, establishing its ownership as the gift of a Count.

Box-wood was the favourite material of the eighteenth-century makers. It had a beautiful texture for turning and carving, and its hardness gave it excellent musical qualities. Staining to a rich red-brown only enhanced its looks, especially when the instrument had ivory mounts.

The outstanding improvement made to the recorder in the eighteenth century was the invention of the double holes for the lowest semitones, low F sharp and G sharp on the treble. For many years it seemed as if the Bressan quartet of recorders in the Grosvenor museum at Chester (Fig. 38) were the only examples of this until the same feature was noticed on another Bressan instrument, a treble in the Kunsthistorisches Museum at Vienna. This not only has the double holes to which we are now accustomed, but also for the third finger of the left hand (Plate VI). What can be the purpose of this? The writer has made experiments with a recorder of similar construction, but these have so far been inconclusive, though the device does make the high D-E trill easier. A

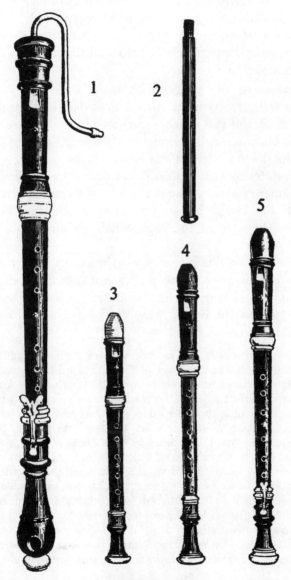

Fig. 38

The 'Chester Recorders' made by Bressan (1) Bass (2) Post to support Bass (3) Treble (4) Alto (5) Tenor, in the Grosvenor Museum, Chester.

similar double hole was usual on oboes of the eighteenth century for the two G sharps and the high D sharp. Although Bressan used the idea of double holes on some of his instruments, examples by other makers of the same period are rare although the idea is clearly shown in Hotteterre's *Principes* in the fingering chart (Fig. 58) and description.

The makers of the sixteenth century, with the exception of Rauch von Schrattenbach, are known to us only by their marks and initials, but at the end of the seventeenth century we find such names as Hotteterre, Drumbleby, Denner, Stanesby, Bressan, Oberlaender, Heytz, Rippert and many others.

The Hotteterres have already been mentioned. Examples of their workmanship are to be found at the Paris Conservatoire, at Leningrad, and in the private collection of Madame Thibault de Chambure. They are of the type which we now describe as the baroque recorder.

The Denners are chiefly famous as the inventors of the clarinet. But their recorders are to be found in many of the museums of Europe, from the beautiful ivory sopranino at Basle (Plate XIV) to basses in Munich (of ivory, Plate VIII), Linz and Nürnberg. Sir John Hawkins wrote:

> 'Johann Christopher Denner is celebrated for his exquisite skill and ingenuity in the construction of flutes, and other instruments of the like kind; he was born at Leipsig on the thirteenth day of August, 1655; and at the age of eight years was taken to Nuremburg, in which city his father, a common turner in wood, had then lately chose to settle with his family. After a very few years stay there, the younger Denner, having been instructed like other boys of his age, in the rudiments of music, betook himself to his father's trade, and in particular to the fabricating of flutes, hautboys, and other wind instruments, which by the help of a nice ear, added to the skill he had acquired in music, and the proficiency he had attained to in playing on them, he tuned so exquisitely, that his instruments were sought for from all parts . . . . He died on the twentieth day of April, 1707, leaving behind two sons who followed the business of their father, and like him, were excellent performers on most of the instruments that they professed to make.'

After these words of praise for Denner's tuning it is a little strange to find on another page the following in a footnote:

> 'There is an objection that lies in common against all perforated pipes; the best that the makers of them can do is to tune them to some one

XX. The writer with Max and Stephanie Champion. *Photo: Dora Head.*

XXI. Frans Bruggen, Beverly Smith, Walter Bergmann and Edgar Hunt playing
Bressan treble recorders

XXII. Carl Dolmetsch tuning and testing a sopranino recorder.
Photo: François Dolmetsch

XXIII. Arnold Dolmetsch, 1858-1940.
Photo: Colin Futcher.

key, as the hautboy to C, the German flute to D, and the flute à bec to
to F; and to effect this truly, is a matter of no small difficulty. The
flutes of the latter kind of the younger Stanesby approach the nearest
of any to perfection; but those of Bressan, though excellent in their
tone, are all too flat in the upper octave. For these reasons some are
induced to think, notwithstanding what we daily hear of a fine
embouchure, and a brilliant finger, terms equally nonsensical applied,
as they are, to the German flute, that the utmost degree of proficiency
on any of these instruments is scarcely worth the labour of attaining it.'

Hawkins never tired of hitting at wind players and flautists in
particular; but it is interesting to read what he said about the two
famous London makers. He was probably quoting a contemporary
opinion.

Eric Halfpenny has done valuable research into the English
eighteenth-century makers and tells us that Thomas Stanesby
(c. 1668-1734) was a native of Derbyshire who came to London
before 1682, becoming a Freeman of the Turners' Company in
1691 and setting up his business in Stonecutter Street.

His son, Thomas II, known as Stanesby Junior (1692-1754), was
apprenticed to his father in 1706. It appears that after working with
his father for a number of years Thomas II set up shop inde-
pendently about 1728 in Fleet Street, near St Dunstan's Church.

The treble in the Carse Collection (Plate XII No. 2) was the
work of Stanesby Senior; his son made the beautiful ivory sixth
flute, carved with vine leaves and a cupid's head (Plate IX).

Peter Bressan was described as 'my good friend' by James
Paisible in his will. Now Paisible was one of those responsible for
introducing the new French woodwind instruments to England
and it seems most likely that Bressan followed him from France.
Eric Halfpenny has found that a Peter Brisson and his wife,
Catharina, were granted Denization in 1683. (The name suffered
many misspellings at the pens of bureaucrats. Lady Jeans has
noted [Galpin Society Journal, May 1958, No. XI] that Brazong
or Brezong was one of the Hoboys who attended King William III
in Holland, about 1690). Dr Maurice Byrne is making further
researches and has found that Bressan came originally from the
district of Bresse (south of Dijon).

In spite of Hawkins's criticism, the writer considers Bressan's
instruments to be Strads among recorders. Examples of his work-

manship are to be found all over Europe as well as in England. There is the famous quartet in Chester (Fig. 38), and in the same museum are to be found another treble and an alto in E flat by him. Bury St. Edmunds museum has an alto in D. Others are known in private hands, including the writer's treble and fourth flute. Then there are a treble and a bass in Prague, a treble in Vienna, and others in Berlin, Paris and The Hague.

The mark on Bressan's instruments has puzzled many. It looks like a tudor rose and PuI Bressan. Thurston Dart has given the best explanation when he compares Jean-Baptiste Loeillet who became John Loeillet of London with a Pierre-Jean Bressan who might have become our Peter Bressan. There is the analogous case of another recorder maker, IoI Schuchart, where the IoI or IuI is probably J-J. Schuchart was a maker of the eighteenth century of whom we have no biographical details. (Plate XII, No. 4).

In the library of Christ Church, Oxford, there is a MS of notes made by James Talbot of Cambridge* about 1685. They give the measurements of all kinds of musical instruments at that time, and include details of tenor and bass recorders made by Bressan. Talbot also gives the pitches of flutes, as follows: Fifth higher (c″). Eighth higher (f″). Voice, third lower (d′). Tenor 5th [sic] lower (c′). Bass (F). Double Bass (C). In his notes the space for the 'treble flute' has not been filled in. These names confirm our English method of nomenclature and it is interesting to note that Talbot chose Bressan instruments as his standard.

A contemporary of the Stanesbys and Bressan was Joseph Bradbury. They all made instruments which we regard as typical of the eighteenth century and of the recorder at its best. One very important difference between the recorders of Bressan, in particular, and modern recorders is the shallow wind-way. Eric Halfpenny has kindly allowed us to reproduce (Plate XIII) one of his X-ray photographs which will show this feature. The picture shows two trebles, one with an ivory ring from the Chester Quartet and one from his own collection. The writer's own Bressan treble is similar but an X-ray would not show the wind-way on account of the ivory mouthpiece.

Even less is known of the lives of most of the other recorder

*Anthony Baines on James Talbot MS, *Galpin Society Journal* No. 1, 1948.

makers between 1660 and 1760, but there seem to have been six main centres of the craft: La Couture and Paris in France, Amsterdam and Brussels in the Low Countries, Berlin and Nürnberg in Germany, in addition to London.

Richard Haka of Amsterdam was actually born in London, but worked in Amsterdam at *De Vergulde Bas-Fluijt,* and died in 1709. There is a descant of his at Leipzig, and at The Hague, a 'walking-stick' recorder—a stick, part of which is hollowed to form a playable recorder.

Jan de Jager (—c. 1694) also worked in Amsterdam, and so did Jan Jurriaens van Heerde (from 1670-79) who probably died in 1691. Langwill quotes the *Amsterdamsch Courant* of that year: 'The widow and son of the late Jan van Heerde, noted in his life as a flute maker at Amsterdam, wish to make known their intention to continue the business of making flutes, oboes, and bassoons.' Two Flemish makers were Jean Hyacinthe Rottenburgh of Brussels, and T. Boekhout, whose bass is shown in Plate XV. Another Amsterdam maker was W. Beukers (c. 1704).

According to Langwill, Robert Wijne of Nijmegen was born in 1698, the son of Hendrik Wijne and Aaltje Timmer, married in 1724 and died in 1774. The treble in the writer's collection (Plate VII) is of box, stained a dark reddish-brown and stamped R. Wyne in a scroll, with a crown above and a double-headed eagle below.

Among the French makers were I. Scherer (c. 1764) and Rippert (c. 1701). Rippert was mentioned with Hotteterre as a most able maker of instruments. (Plate VIII).

Berlin is represented by Heitz, or Heytz (Plate XII); and, besides the Denners, Nürnberg can boast of Franziskus Kynsker and J. W. Oberlaender (c. 1760). Kynsker was the maker of the fine set of seven recorders shown in Plate VII.

After the recorder had been outsted from professional and fashionable amateur circles by the German flute, the makers, who retained their skill in voicing these instruments, tried to attract the amateurs by bringing out a number of 'novelty' instruments with 'whistle' mouthpieces. To the amateur the flute was more difficult then the recorder because of its *embouchure*—the placing and control of the lips which have to do all that the recorder's wind-way does and more. So the first thing to do was to construct a side-blown recorder (Plate XVII, No. 4). The example shown has the four keys which were added to the flute at this time. This is reminiscent of the *Dolzflöten* of Praetorius (Fig. 12).

The so-called 'voice flute' (Plate XVII No. 1), is held like a recorder, but has the key mechanism of a six-keyed flute in order to produce the semitones without cross-fingerings (the holes are in any case too large for cross-fingerings to be effective).

Bainbridge never tired of bringing out new inventions and patents. Such were the little English flageolet (Plate XVII No. 2) with its key for producing the semitones, and the two little keys at the foot—presumably 'Quantz keys'—one for D sharp and the other for E flat! Ever since the ancient Greeks played the *diaulos* people have been fascinated by the idea of double pipes (see Plates II No. 6 and XIV No. 1). The double flageolet panders to this idea and enjoyed a vogue at the beginning of the nineteenth century. The example shown on Plate XVII is beautifully made and tuned. Both the flageolets, 2 and 3 in this plate, have the bulbous chamber at the top of the instrument, below the little ivory mouthpiece, which is designed to take a sponge to absorb the moisture from the player's breath. This was a feature of the flageolets, but seems never to have been adopted for the recorder, unless Burney was in fact referring to one when he wrote of a person 'who plays on the common flute in a particular manner, blowing it thro' a sponge' (*Music, Men and Manners in France and Italy* 1770).

These musical toys had their day, but there were no lasting qualities to aid their survival. They were neither recorders nor flutes, and had no proper music of their own, nor any place in the scheme of musical ensembles. So today they are only antique curiosities. Let them be a lesson to the inventors of novelty instruments.

6

RECORDER TECHNIQUE

The technique of playing a musical instrument is something which is built up over a period of time and handed down from teacher to pupil. With each generation some outworn ideas are discarded and some new features added, but through the whole flows the mainstream of tradition. Only occasionally does a teacher commit to print the secrets of his art: but when he does, his book becomes a valuable document.

Technique is constantly changing under the influence of a number of factors. It is influenced by musical taste, by the parallel development of other arts, of other instruments and their techniques; by improvements and changes in the design and making of instruments. We must not fall into the nineteenth-century way of regarding this always as progress; but at least we learn from history, from the successes as well as the mistakes of the past—and then we make our own mistakes as well as our improvements.

In the case of the recorder, the books of Ganassi and of Hotteterre tell us something of how the recorder was played in 1535 and 1707 respectively, and a number of other books give fingering charts. But the tradition of recorder playing was lost in the nineteenth century, and we now have to develop it anew. It is not enough to try and play like Ganassi or Hotteterre. To do that would be to put back the clock. Instead we must build a twentieth-century technique, learning as much as possible from the past, and imagining a continuous development parallel to that of the oboe or flute, which have not suffered a comparable break in tradition.

In doing this we must consider first of all the nature of our instrument and how it differs from its fellows. The oboe, flute and recorder were equals at the beginning of the eighteenth century; so equal, in fact, that Hotteterre was able to write for them together in both his books. At that time the flute was eager for development. It had one key (the equivalent of the double holes which the recorder had acquired), but others were soon added for the semitones, with foot keys to extend the compass downwards. Why were these keys necessary? Because the flute operates on a higher wind-pressure than the recorder, and such a higher pressure sharpens the cross-fingered notes more than the plain ones. Also there was a demand for bigger tone, and larger finger-holes served to provide that, but at the same time made it impossible to produce semitones by cross-fingerings. In the case of the oboe semitones could be produced very well by means of cross-fingering. The oboe was loud enough and the tone of the forked notes was really more pleasant than that of the open ones. Larger finger-holes were not wanted, as they would only have made the tone more blatant. But the keys did serve to make the tone more even, and the invention of octave keys helped to extend the range of the instrument (they do the work of our thumb—'pinched notes').

In the 1840s Theobald Boehm of Munich completely revolutionized the flute and its technique. He gave it an almost cylindrical bore and very large finger-holes—so large that they all had to be covered by means of an elaborate key mechanism. This made the flute more equal in power to the oboe and clarinet, and more useful in the orchestra. Some features of the Boehm keymechanism were borrowed for the oboe and clarinet—such as the idea of ring keys—but they were otherwise unaffected.

How about the recorder? The recorder is the *flauto dolce,* and is voiced on a fairly low wind pressure. Unless it is overblown, the cross-fingerings do very well to provide the semitones to complete its chromatic scale. If we wanted to make the recorder more powerful, we should probably have to enlarge the bore and enlarge the finger-holes. The first would probably limit the compass (unless possibly coupled with a system of octave keys), the second would destroy the forked notes and make semitone keys necessary. The flautist can adjust his lips to play over three octaves: the recorder has a fixed wind-way, and it would need a Boehm to think of a way of modifying that. Some modifications have been thought of and applied, and these are discussed in Chapter 8. Meanwhile we must take the recorder as it is, and consider what is involved in its technique, and what we can learn from history and from other instruments today.

Holding the recorder

This is obviously the first heading to be discussed. As to the angle at which it should be held, there have been slight variations over the ages and according to the size of the instrument. The writer recommends that it should be held well up, at an angle of between 45° and 65° to the vertical, so that the player looks alert, and the instrument rests on his right-hand thumb. It is deplorable to see how some school children and adults droop over their instruments—a fault often started in the classroom by trying to read music on the near-flat top of a desk. This fault can be traced back to the time of Ganassi (look at his picture Fig. 3) and to the Elizabethan method of printing music 'consort-way'* (when the separate parts were printed *tête-bêche,* so that the players could read their parts from a single copy sitting round a table). A music stand is an essential piece of equipment.

The *Stützfingertechnik* (supporting—or buttress-finger technique) of the eighteenth century, which has been revived by F. J. Giesbert in his *Schule für die Altblockflöte,* has a bearing on this question of holding. The idea was to provide some extra support for the instrument by adding the third finger of the right hand for some notes, and this idea can be traced in the fingering charts from the time of Hudgebut onwards to the end of the eighteenth century. The disadvantage is that the player has to remember *which* notes and ensure that the extra finger does not spoil a note for which it is not required! Besides, the third is supposed to be a weak finger, and this use of it is cramping to the hand-position. Instead, the writer advises the use of the fourth finger, which, when not otherwise occupied in closing the lowest hole, can rest on the beading between the two lowest holes. This corresponds to the use of the same finger on the D sharp key of the flute—an essential part of flute technique. It not only gives support but helps in the location of the right-hand fingers after a passage in which they have not been involved.

A thumb rest is an advantage on a tenor recorder, particularly if the latter has a key for the low C which prevents the use of the fourth finger for support as just described. This rest can be of the type used for clarinets. It ought not to be necessary for a treble or smaller instrument.

How should you hold the mouthpiece of the recorder? Some

---

*This method was tried by the present writer in *A Practical Method,* as he wished to provide the separate parts of quintets without a number of separate sheets which could get lost. The idea was not continued, and such quintets are now printed in score.

hold it between the lips only; others, including the writer, prefer a more secure hold. Draw the lower lip over the lower teeth to form a cushion on which to rest the beak of the recorder: the upper teeth can then rest on the top of the mouthpiece, while the upper lip is wrapped round to make all air-tight. It is important to have a firm hold so as to leave the fingers as free as possible. If the recorder is held in front of the teeth, there is always the risk that the upper teeth might get in the way of the breath stream.

The bass recorders generally need different treatment. Basses which are blown direct need only a slight modification of the normal position; but all the others need special treatment. It is best to take the weight of the instrument from the player's fingers by means of a sling passing round the player's neck and attached to the ring (which is often incorporated in a thumb-rest, as on a bass clarinet or saxophone). Bressan's basses* were often provided with a post which fitted into the end of the instrument and rested on the floor—an ideal method when the player was seated. The post was adjustable telescopically, and was hollow—which probably served to add a little resonance. The foot-joint of the instrument itself was made so that the acoustical end of the tube was at the side (Fig. 38). Most players hold the instrument diagonally across the body with the foot of the instrument to the right (seated, with the foot to the right of the right thigh), though the writer personally prefers to hold it straight in front (seated, between the legs) like Hudgebut's left-hand angel! (Fig. 23.)

The great bass may be held diagonally when standing, but is probably easier to hold straight in front when seated. It is a good idea to provide it with a very short 'end-pin'—like a 'cello—to support it off the ground when seated.

Left or right hand?

Nowadays we take it for granted that a woodwind instrument should be played with the left hand uppermost. This was not always so and, as we have already explained, *la flûte à neuf trous* had its origin in this indecision. Between 1528 and 1545 Agricola made up his mind on the subject. In the 1528 edition of *Musica Instrumentalis Deudsch* he wrote:

---

*Also one by T. Boekhout at the Leningrad Institute for Theatre, Music and Cinematography (Plate XV).

*Nim die pfeiffe zum aller ersten mal
Ynn beyde hend/und solt haben die wal.
Welche hand du wilt/solt oben halden
Die ander sol allzeit unten walden.

But in 1545 that was changed to:

†Sol dir di kunst werden bekand   Darzu wird es sein von nöten
So nim die Pfeiff also zurhand   das das underst loch auff flöten
Die recht oben die linck unden   Zur rechten ungegriffen bleybt
So hastu den angriff funden/   Und mit wachsse werd zugekleybt.

Ganassi, to judge by the frontispiece of *Fontegara,* was undecided; as that picture shows two players with the left hand uppermost and one the other way. Jambe de Fer devotes most of his space to explaining the purpose of the ninth hole; but in his fingering chart the left-hand hole is shown 'stopt with wax'.

Hotteterre le Romain was quite definite: 'On posera la Main gauche en haut, & la droite en bas, comme on le voit demontré.' (Fig. 19).

But by making the recorder with an adjustable foot-joint, his family had made possible the continuance of left-handed playing.

Left-handed playing must have persisted in England well into the eighteenth century. When, in 1949, the writer examined the Chester recorders and played on them, he found them a little uncomfortable to manage on account of the way in which the thumb-holes were worn. When tried with the right hand uppermost they were much easier. Then he noted that the double holes were tilted a little as if for left-handed players.

In the case of other woodwind instruments: one-keyed flutes were adjustable, but players' minds were made up for them as soon as further keys were added, and this put an end to the left-handed hold. In the case of oboes, the low C key was provided with a 'butterfly' touch while the D sharp key was duplicated; but the left-hand touch of the C key was retained, being a pleasing design, for some time after the left-hand D sharp key had disappeared.

---

*Take the pipe for the first time
in both hands. You have the choice
which hand you want to have above.
The other one shall always reign below.

†If you want to learn the art
take the pipe in the following way into
your hands:
the right one above, the left below.
Thus you have made a beginning.
It will also be necessary
not to finger the lowest hole
of the recorder on the right-hand side,
but to close it with wax.

The clarinet was not invented until about 1690 when left-handed playing should have been on the way out; and yet there are ambidexterous examples. The present writer has a clarinette d'amour by I.S.W. (? Walch of Berchtesgaden) with duplicate holes for F(c) (a peg is provided for stopping the unwanted one), a centrally placed G sharp (d sharp) key, and a thumb key (placed centrally on the under side) for the low E(b).

A few recorder players even today say they are left handed, and order special instruments. It is possibly an advantage for a teacher, as members of his class would see him mirror-wise, eliminating the need to translate left into right. Others again adopt the left-handed hold through an accident to one of the right-hand fingers. But these are exceptions, and it is better for recorder players to do the same as players of the flute, oboe or clarinet in this matter.

Breathing

Having decided how to hold the recorder, the next topic for discussion is breathing. Ganassi and other writers tell us to emulate singers; but that was at a time when singers were the very cream of the musical profession, and when instrumental music was largely dependent on vocal. Since those days instrumental music has advanced so considerably that in matters of technique the balance may be said to be reversed, and it is quite as important to study our fellow instrumentalists.

In playing the recorder we must begin with a good breath supply, using the diaphragm as the controlling muscle. Now here there is a basic difference between playing the recorder and, for instance, the oboe, clarinet or flute. In the case of these latter three, the breath pressure meets the resistance of the reed or of the player's lips, and this resistance supports the breath column. In the case of the recorder the application of similar pressure would result in an unbearably harsh tone quality, and would also entail the use of far too much breath, as the wind-way of the instrument is too large to offer a comparable resistance. So the breath, instead of being forced through the mouthpiece, has to be controlled entirely from the diaphragm.

To find the right pressure, try blowing too hard as well as too softly until you find the point between the two extremes where the tone is pleasant but firm. If you let the breath pressure drop too low, your tone will be dull and lifeless. If the breathing comes from the diaphragm the tone will never be dead. A number of recorders blown too harshly produces a terrible sound, and in fear of this teachers cause their pupils to blow so feebly that they never fill their instruments properly. By now you will have found that if you try to play *f*, your note will be harsh and sharp in pitch: if you try to play *p* it will be flat and lifeless; so keep to your *mf* and your tone will be more flexible, and you will be able to play a little louder or softer without upsetting your intonation, according to the needs of the music.

If the music asks you to play loudly, you must take away the harshness and sharpness by introducing an undulation known as 'vibrato'. The following diagram (Fig. 39) will help to show how this is accomplished:

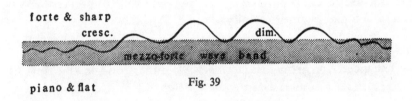

forte & sharp
cresc.   dim.
mezzoforte wave band
piano & flat   Fig. 39

In this, the crests of the waves are *f* and sharp, but the listener accepts the sound as 'in tune' because the valleys remain within the in-tune *mf* wave band. Note for comparison that the vibrato of a good string player is between the note and something sharp of that note (not a wobble on both sides of the note); and, similarly, one of the organ's vibrato effects consists of an out-of-tune pipe which causes 'beats'—the *vox angelica* or the *voix celeste*—a pipe which is sharp to the pitch of the organ.

How is this vibrato produced? Singers use the diaphragm, and this is all right as long as it is controlled. The singer's vibrato, started at the diaphragm, has to be effective at the vocal cords, about 12" away. Now, if the recorder player uses this form of vibrato, it has to be effective at the mouthpiece of the instrument, and that is about 6" farther.

In England at least, many players use a form of throat vibrato, which can be controlled in speed and is effective. The distance involved is no more than about 6", and it can be likened to the tremulant of an organ. It consists of a series of silent Hs (as if saying 'ha, ha, ha, ha,' silently and fairly quickly). Much breath is wasted and ink spilt in attacking this form of vibrato, by people who have not troubled to study its possibilities. They call it a 'goat's trill'. Obviously this method of disturbing the breath stream is of no use to the singer. But recorder players are not singers; and although there may be some similarities between their aims, they do not necessarily have to employ the same techniques. For recorder playing it is important to provide a steady breath supply, and that is the duty of the diaphragm. Any modifications to that supply can be produced, like the tremulant of the organ, in the wind trunk. If the recorder needed a higher breath pressure, like the oboe, then the diaphragm vibrato might be better. Whichever method is used, the speed of the vibrato must be controlled. Too fast a vibrato is most undesirable. So also is one that is too slow. Do not use it when playing softly, but reserve it to prevent harshness when playing more loudly.

Tongueing

The need for articulation was fully understood in the time of Ganassi, and assumed as an essential element of technique. Just as in speech, consonants are used to give shape to the vowels, so certain consonants are used by wind players to phrase the music. The tongue restrains the breath, to release it at the precise moment demanded by the music; and the exact form of the tongue's movement is suggested by the consonants selected. Suitable consonants include: T, K, D, G, L and R (unrolled). T and D both use the tip of the tongue, K and G the back. T and K use a higher breath pressure and give a more precise attack than D and G. Then there are the TH and TLE sounds which are also useful. The 'flutter-tongue' effect, produced by rolling the tongue, has found a place in recorder music, notably to imitate to cooing of the dove in Britten's *Noye's Fludde*. This effect is more difficult of produce on the recorder, with its low breath pressure, than, for instance, on the flute; and some players may find it easier if the mouth is opened a little to reduce the pressure.

Music consists of related sounds and must flow: so it is wise to think of the tongue's action, not so much like a gas tap being turned on and off, but rather like the stick which keeps a child's hoop in motion, or like a footballer's foot dribbling the ball across a field. Think of the notes of a melody as a string of pearls: they are strung together and they are graded; the notes are articulated just as each pearl on that string is a separate sphere; but they are linked by the thread. Think of a series of articulated notes, not so much like a broken necklace, but like that string of pearls, where each one is separated by a knot—they are separate, and yet they belong.

A lot of twentieth-century recorder teaching goes wrong through an over-insistence on tongueing. Tunes are desiccated in this way. So the meaning of the slur should be taught as well, right from the start. In music for wind instruments, when two or more notes are slurred together, the first is tongued, but the others under that slur are to be played in the same uninterrupted breath. In writing music the slur should never be used to cover the whole phrase (as some careless composers use it) unless it is really intended that the phrase in question should be played without any articulation. 'Phrasing' can always be shown by the right use of breath marks, if the music does not already make it clear enough. So it behoves all composers and arrangers to be exact in their markings of slurs, etc.

Staccato in its varying degrees mean to the player 'tongue each note'—there will naturally be degrees of shortness. It does not mean attack the beginning of a note, but rather shorten the end of it. *Legato* to the player means slur. *Mezzo-staccato* (shown by dots under a slur .⌢.) means tongue each note so gently that the effect is almost legato. Some people use the contradictory term 'tongued legato' when they really mean *mezzo-staccato*.

Looking back on the history of this branch of technique, we have already noted that Ganassi advised the use of a variety of consonants, and paired them for double-tongueing as: TK, DK, TR, DR, KR, and LR. These he wrote out with different vowels as: Taka teke tiki toko tuku; though the vowel makes no difference to the resulting note any more than it makes any difference whether a pianist uses his finger or a pencil to depress the key—it only affects the comfort of the player.* The choice of vowel can, however, indirectly influence a performance. Imagine a player who holds his

---

*This was demonstrated by Mr Antony Hopkins at a conference of the I.S.M. While the pundits were debating what kind of touch he was using to play the melody of a Chopin Nocturne, he was using a pencil held in his teeth for the purpose.

head too high and shapes his mouth for an E sound. The muscles of his throat and face will be tense and his tone likely to be hard (possibly accompanied by a grunt in the throat). It would be better to hold the head down, relax and open the throat as if saying AW. 'Double tongueing' is necessary when the music is too quick for the player to make the repeated T T T or D D D strokes with the tongue: he then uses a balanced movement involving the alternate use of different parts of the tongue: T K (tip and back), L R (using different parts of the middle of the tongue). These ideas were already established when Agricola told his recorder player to 'lern wol das *diri diride'*.

Hotteterre used *tü* as his normal tongueing syllable and *tü rü* tongueing, often putting the *rü* in the stronger position. His aim was to give the pairs of notes the iambic inequality which was characteristic of French music at the end of the seventeenth century.

Today, for double tongueing on the recorder, the following are generally used: T K, D G, and T TL. With the light breath-pressure of the recorder T K is often too explosive, and D G is found to be better, though it is also effective to 'tootle' on your flute when your flute is a recorder. For dotted rhythms the TH syllable is useful, as in the following examples (Fig. 40):

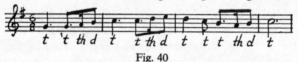

Fig. 40

Phrasing

Breathing and tongueing are both the servants of what can best be described as phrasing. In the past this has not been indicated by composers with sufficient accuracy and thought for the final effect, and many modern editions of eighteenth-century sonatas need revision.

So much of phrasing is a matter of individual preference that it is difficult to lay down rules, but the writer finds himself constantly telling his pupils:

1. Never take breath on a bar line, unless you have a very good reason for doing so.
2. Never take breath before a long or important note. There may be a *silence d'articulation* before such a note, but such a gap should not be used for breath.

110

3. Be very cautious about slurring 'weak to strong';

 might be a French overture, but
is a tune by Dvorak. Such slurring was rare in the eighteenth century although examples can be found, as in Barsanti's C major sonata.

4. Breathe after a long note unless that long note happens to be a suspension. If the latter, resolve the suspension first. There may sometimes have to be exceptions in the 'Air on the G String' type of melody, where there is an elaborate ornamental resolution.

5. If you want to accent a note, don't hit it harder, but rather lighten the notes before it. Remember that if you tongue too strongly, you will get more spit and less note!

Ornamentation

This is a subject which arises here because the greater part of recorder music belongs to the eighteenth century, and this was a period when the Italian style settled like a blight on much that was fine in music.

Ornamentation can be separated into the conventional trills at cadences and other ornaments that are indicated in the music on the one hand; and on the other, the runs and colorature that a highly skilled player may add as a kind of artistic exuberance. Such embellishments must grow out of the music, and not sound like 'ornaments' superimposed on a perfectly good tune, like fretwork stuck on a piece of Victorian furniture.

In considering this matter of ornamentation we must remember its context. It came with the rise of the Concert Hall, with the appearance of the professional virtuoso as distinct from the sincere musician. It was no longer the enjoyment of the music which came first, but the showing off of a skilful player. Difficulty had become more important than quality. So if the ornamentation you propose to add falls naturally and genuinely ornaments the music, by all means play it: if it sounds artificial or originates from a desire to show off, it is vulgar and better not played. Here there is a very useful motto: 'when in doubt, leave out'.

Some of the books written for the benefit of examination students give the abbreviations of the ornaments of the Beethoven period quite clearly but are vague about the earlier styles, so recorder players may find the following notes helpful:

1. All trills start on the upper note. All good rules have exceptions, and you can start your trill on the printed note when it is approached from below, and sometimes when it is preceded by the upper note:

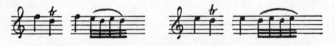

Fig. 42

2. Some trills end with an anticipation of the next note. This is usual at cadences. Other trills will need to be finished with a turn. Others again will merge into the plain note.

Fig. 43

3. Appoggiature are important in eighteenth-century music. They may be generally added at cadences before the trill. An appoggiatura to a dotted note takes two-thirds of its value:

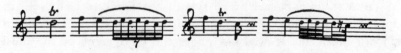

Fig. 44

4. A turn is often written out in time value, slower than the speed of the trill. Try and play it as if it was all part of the trill, not as if the turn was a separate ornament stuck on at the end.

XXIV. Gustav Scheck,
Freiburg

XXV. Ferdinand Conrad, Hanover

XXVI. Carl Dolmetsch and
Jean Henry

PLATES XXVII, XXVIII, XXIX, XXX

(Top Left): Joannes Collette, Nijmegen. *(Top Right):* Kurt Pitsch, Linz-Donau. *(Bottom Left):* Kees Otten, Amsterdam. *(Bottom Right):* The first quartet of recorders to be played in Germany in the present revival—in costume, at Essen-Ruhr in 1928. Instruments by G. H. Hüller of Schöneck (Saxony) and Peter Harlan of Markneukirchen.

Fig. 45

To learn more about this subject in more detail the student should consult Thurston Dart's *The Interpretation of Music* (Hutchinson) Dannreuther's *Musical Ornamentation* (Novello, out of print), Arnold Dolmetsch's *The Interpretation of the Music of the XVII and XVIII Centuries* (Novello) and Robert Donington's *Interpretation of Early Music* (Faber) or, better still, study the old writers themselves.

Fingering

The fingering of the recorder has not changed greatly from the sixteenth century to the present day. To understand it we must look into some of the acoustical principles on which the instrument is constructed, and consider how the vibrating air in the tube behaves.

Blowing down the wind-way formed between the fipple and the inner wall of the recorder's beak, the player's breath is directed against the sharp edge of the instrument's lip. This sets up vibrations known as 'edge tones' which can be heard. These vibrations are transmitted to the air in the recorder; and here we meet the rule— 'the longer the tube, the lower the note'. Covering all holes for the bottom f' of the treble recorder uses the full length of the tube. Lifting one finger to play g', corresponds to using a shorter tube—and so on. In general this is how the first octave and a note are formed.

What about b' flat, f" and g"? To understand how they are formed, we must look at the vibration patterns in the tube. To do this it is helpful to compare what happens inside a wind instrument (which we cannot see) with the vibrations of a string, as on a violin, violoncello or guitar (which we can).

The free part of a violin string is 'fixed' at its two ends where they pass over the nut and the bridge respectively. Sound it with a bow or pluck it, and it will vibrate after the pattern of Fig. 46.

Fig. 46

The crosses mark the points of (comparative) rest or 'nodes', and in the middle there is maximum vibration (or an 'antinode'). Now there cannot very well be points of rest at the lip and at the open end of the recorder, especially as the vibration starts at the lip. In fact the point of rest (node) is about half-way up the tube (Fig. 47), rather as if we had taken the violin pattern, cut it in

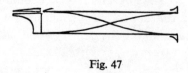

Fig. 47

half, and stuck the two halves, end to end, in the tube (Fig. 48).

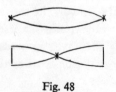

Fig. 48

But what has this to do with b′ flat? Compared with bottom f′, the b′ flat pattern has moved up the tube and is a little smaller (Fig. 49), but it does not stop at the third hole. You can imagine the pattern continued down the tube to another nodal point (dotted line). This may be described as the 'end vibration'.

114

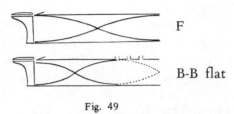

F

B-B flat

Fig. 49

Take the head joint of your recorder, and see what note you get from it. Cup your hand loosely round the end of it, and you will get a flatter note. In doing this you are influencing this 'end vibration'. Go back to your (complete) recorder. If you open the first three holes from the bottom (closing the others) you will get a note midway between b' and b' flat. Leave the third hole open but close all the others again, and you will have flattened that out-of-tune note into a good b' flat.

A recorder's finger holes correspond to tubes of different lengths, like a row of organ pipes, combined into one instrument. If each finger hole were of the same diameter as the bore of the instrument the analogy would be perfect. This, however, is impossible, as the average finger could not cover such large holes; so they are made smaller. As smaller holes give flatter notes, they are moved farther up the instrument (nearer the mouthpiece) to compensate for this.

The frets on a guitar are placed at semitone intervals on the fingerboard, and they get closer together as they go along the string, from the head towards the bridge. Similarly the distances between the holes on the recorder tend to do the same (although this would be more obvious if the bore were not an inverted cone, and all the holes were of the same size).

Applying this to the recorder, you get most of the semitones in the lower octave by missing one hole and covering the next two (to flatten the open note). In the case of b' flat this is adequate, as the first-finger note is already half-way there. In the case of c" flat (which is how b' natural is formed), the first-finger hole is made rather small, so that two fingers are sufficient, although on baroque instruments a third finger also is needed. Going up, d" flat (=c"

115

sharp) often needs the closing of two-and-a-half fingers, using one of the double holes for R.H.3. c″ flat is about right (possibly a little flat, with L.H. thumb, 1 and 3: R.H. 1); but when you reach f″, only one finger is needed to flatten the f″ sharp that you get with the thumb only; two fingers here would give an alternative e″. L.H.2 is used to produce g″: this not only steadies the recorder, but keeps the note under control. If recorders were made with an open g″ (without this finger), some other way of holding the instrument would have to be evolved. The normal f″ sharp is produced by adding L.H. 1 to flatten the last note. Remembering that 'the smaller the hole the flatter the note', the function of the double holes for low g′ flat and a′ flat can be readily understood.

So much for the first octave and a note of fundamentals. In most wind instruments it is possible to obtain higher notes as harmonics of these lower notes, and the recorder is no exception. Here again it will be helpful to compare the vibration patterns of stringed instruments with those of recorders (Fig. 50).

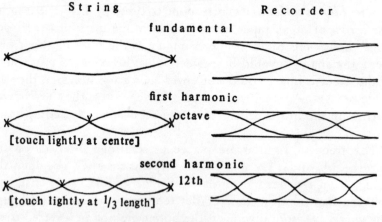

Fig. 50

The recorder, like the flute and oboe, 'over-blows' at the octave. But, as the harder you blow your recorder, the sharper is the note that you get, simple over-blowing will not do. So, how are these harmonics to be produced?

Looking at the first two 'wind' diagrams on the right hand side, the most obvious difference between them is the fact that the pattern for the fundamental has a node half-way along the tube, whereas the first harmonic has maximum vibration at that point. Using this fact we can 'assist' the production of upper notes by disturbing the air in the tube near this point to prevent the formation of a node there. A slight leak near this point will so disturb the vibration pattern that it will change from 'fundamental' to 'first harmonic' with almost the same breath pressure. We cause this leak by pressing the thumb-nail into the thumb hole, so that a very small but controllable chink is exposed. In a scientifically-designed recorder there would have to be a row of these thumb holes, each exactly half-way along the tube for each note; but, as nature has provided us with only one left-hand thumb each, we have to be content with one hole, placed in an average position.

The normal fingering for f" serves for all occasions except for the trill from e" flat. In the case of g" an octave fingering will only exceptionally be required (for the g"–a" and g"–a" flat trills), so the first diatonic octave that we require is for a". The same method is used for c''' and d'''.

So far we have left out b" flat, and here we must notice what happens to the end vibration:

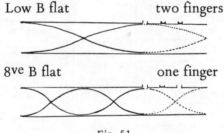

Fig. 51

From this diagram we see that it is shorter for the octave than for the fundamental, and that one finger less will be required for its production. In fact, two fingers would pull it down to a" (=b" double flat). Even this comes in handy for the g"–a" trill. This new pattern 'miss a hole and cover one', also provides us with fingerings for c''' flat (=b") and d''' flat (=c''' sharp).

In our progress with octave harmonics we have left out a" flat (=g" sharp). Now if we try a normal octave harmonic from low g', we find that it is much too sharp for use as g"; but we can sharpen this note still further, by lifting off the left hand thumb and first finger, to provide a good g" sharp.

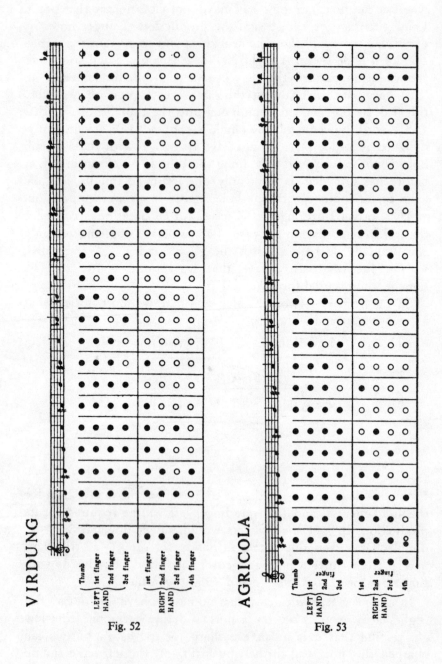

VIRDUNG

Fig. 52

AGRICOLA

Fig. 53

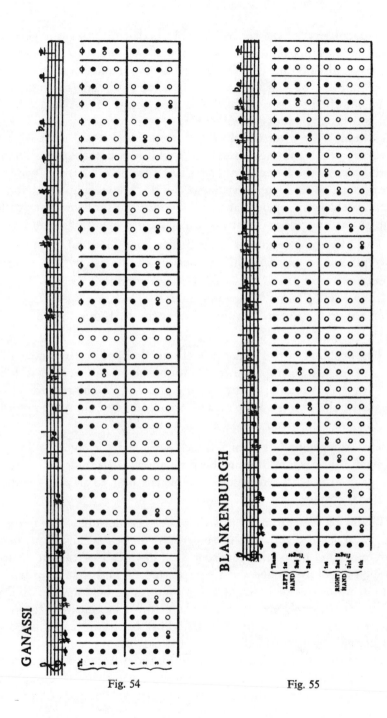

GANASSI

BLANKENBURGH

Fig. 54

Fig. 55

A pecularity of the recorder's bore is that it reacts strangely on some of these harmonics. The octave c″–c‴ may be in tune; but we have already noted that g′–g″ is impossible, and that even a′–a″ tends to be sharp at the top on some recorders (the taper has to be modified to correct this). The next octave, d″–d‴, is slightly flat at the top (and generally needs some correction by opening the thumb-hole after the note has been struck); and after d″ the octaves stop. The next note e‴ will not come as an octave harmonic, as the bore for that part of the recorder is too wide in proportion to its length. An organ builder knows that a wide-bore pipe (such as an open diapason) favours the fundamental, while one of narrower bore (gamba or dulciana) is richer in harmonics.

This e‴ comes easily as a twelfth from a′, assisted (vented) in two places, to prevent the formation of nodes, by the thumb ('pinched') and L.H.3. This fingering is modified to give e‴ flat (adding R.H.3) and f‴ (opening L.H.2). The top g‴ is a fifteenth from the low g′, vented in three places (by L.H. thumb and 2, and R.H.2).

The problem note f‴ sharp is obtained either by flattening g‴, by still further raising e‴ into e‴ double sharp (no wonder it does not want to sound!), or by closing the end of the recorder (by means of the player's knee or with a special key). On some recorders the fingering given by Majer can be used.

The exceptional fingerings which we need for some trills, are derived either by modifying the note above (flattening it) or from the printed note. To remember them it is best to classify them as one or the other.

It will be seen from all this that the recorder obeys the natural law of acoustics, and that its fingerings can be logically explained. Anyone who plays the recorder one day realizes that it is not enough to blow evenly and finger correctly; and that in order to get 26 notes out of its eight holes there must be some flexibility of breath control, and that the player must be sensitive to pitch and tone quality, and be able to adjust breathing and fingering readily according to the dictates of the ear.

In comparing the fingerings given by the different writers, from Virdung onwards, various points should be noticed. In compiling the charts the earlier ones have been given on the basis of a tenor

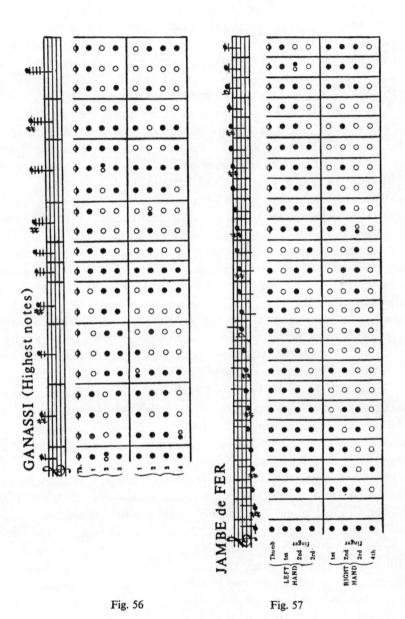

Fig. 56　　　　　　　Fig. 57

121

recorder in C: those after Hotteterre for a treble in F—the standard instrument of the eighteenth century.

Virdung (Fig. 52) offers a limited compass—up to b" flat. He does not employ half-coverings; so there is no low c' sharp. His semitones are given on a basis of 'miss a hole and cover one' (not two) in both octaves. Were his octaves in tune? Note the c" sharp with the thumb as on a 'penny whistle', and the open d".

Agricola (Fig. 53) shows an advance by giving the half-covering for the low c' sharp (he uses a special sign for this). The chart is built up from the best of both editions, but neither gives the upper c" sharp. The two Fs are the reverse of what one would expect. The compass is now extended to b" natural.

Ganassi's chart (Fig. 54) is a composite one. In his *Fontegara* he gives the fingerings for a number of different scales (or modes) and G sharp in one will differ from A flat in another, and so on. His fingerings for the notes beyond the two octaves are given in a separate table (Fig. 56). He makes full use of half-coverings for the low semitones, also for g' sharp and many other higher notes. His fingering for c" sharp gives d" on the instruments the writer has tried, but his fingerings for the very high notes are remarkably successful on a replica of a sixteenth-century tenor. For a fuller statement of these fingerings the reader should consult Dr Hildemarie Peter's edition of the original.

Jambe de Fer's chart (Fig. 57) shows that the fingerings are settling down to a pattern. He dispenses with the low c' sharp, but is there a mistake in the higher one? The fingering would work if the thumb were left open—but it is firmly closed in his chart! All these early books have to be taken E & OE.

Blankenburgh (Fig. 55) (and van Eyck), about a century later, marks the end of the sixteenth-century recorder. But here's a highly original plan. There is no chart in the original: Blankenburgh and van Eyck both describe—just as Hotteterre did—the fingers to be raised for each note, and this chart is the result of following their directions. The unusual feature of this is the great use made of half-coverings in place of the more usual cross-fingerings. Where both are given, the implication is that the 'sharp' is flatter than the corresponding 'flat'.

Hotteterre (Fig. 58) is the representative of countless others, including the English 'Companions'. Here is the *Stützfinger*

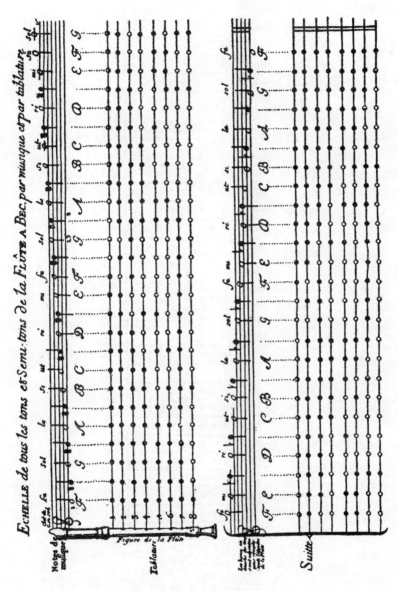

Fig. 58. Hotteterre's Fingerings

123

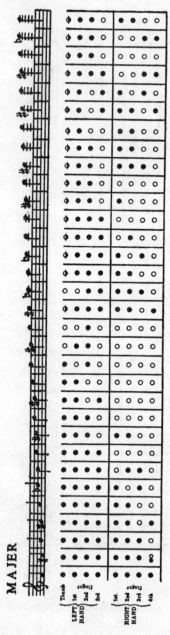

Fig. 59

124

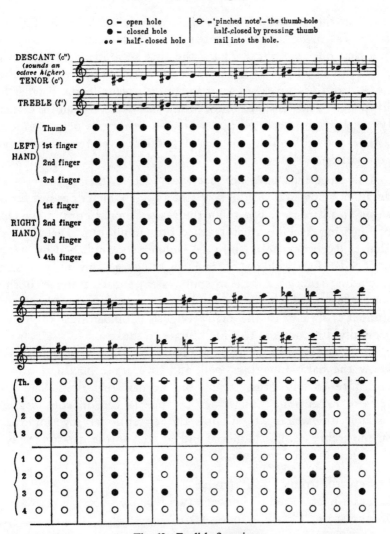

Fig. 60. English fingerings

Technik and a fingering approaching that of today: the main difference being the matter of the Bs and B flats. Did Jambe de Fer anticipate this *Stützfinger* in his B flat and C?

Majer (Fig. 59) is interesting as he gives fingerings for the highest notes. He has given up the idea of *Stützfinger Technik*, ventures a high F sharp and, apart from his low G sharp and B flat, would do today. Adam Carse, when writing about fingerings dismissed Majer as too inaccurate. On examining the copy of Majer's book in the British Museum, the writer found that the fingering chart was made up of a number of wood blocks, fitted together, and that one section, involving the first six notes, had been printed upside-down, making nonsense of them. Degen omitted these notes from his book, as he, too, could not understand what had happened! The facsimile shows the chart correctly, and is evidently taken from a later edition where the error has been corrected.

The normal English fingering (Fig. 60) is given for reference and comparison.

Trill fingerings have not been included in this chapter in any detail as being outside the scope of a book which does not set out to be an instructor. For them the reader should consult the chart of fingering issued by Schott & Co Ltd (London) or Part III of the School Recorder Book, by Carl Dolmetsch, published by Arnold of Leeds. Early charts of trill fingerings are given by Ganassi (including trills of a third in some cases) and Hotteterre, both of which are available in facsimile and should be in the serious student's library. In the many English 'Companions' there were generally directions as to which finger to shake.

In order to build up a sound technique, the player is advised to know the basic fingerings well, and to practise playing from any one note to any other, using the normal fingerings. Then add certain 'exceptional' fingerings for use in certain contexts. For instance, the writer would allow the 'exceptional fingering' for e″ on the treble (L. H. thumb, 2 and 3) (b″ on the descant) only in the following circumstances:

1. for a trill from e″ to f″ (treble),
2. for an unaccented e″ between two f″s,
3. for a strong f″ falling to a weak e″.

a. never use it on a strong beat as it is slightly sharp on most instruments:
b. Never use it when you are just too lazy to use the normal fingering.

Unless the player has a definite plan of fingering, he will never be a reliable sight-reader, as he will be for ever tossing up as to which fingering to use!

The experienced player will find fingering can aid expression, and will become accustomed to 'shading' a note if it is too sharp, or 'opening' one that is too flat; and in this instance it is better to regard certain fingerings as modifications of a normal fingering for a particular purpose, rather than as separate alternatives. But these are matters for the advanced students which can only be taught as circumstances dictate. In his *Il flauto dolce ed acerbo* Michael Vetter has explored these alternatives in great detail, including those obtainable with the end of the recorder covered and closed. *Avant garde* composers make great use of these alternative fingerings together with 'chords' which can be obtained by over-blowing, as well as various forms of flutter tongueing and vibrato, singing while playing, glissando effects, and even the gentle percussive sound of fingers on holes.

7

THE REVIVAL OF THE RECORDER

The present revival of the recorder and its wide use as an educational instrument had its beginnings towards the end of the nineteenth century. Interest in musical instruments at that time worked in two directions. On the one hand, there were those like Sax and Boehm who evolved new instruments or who tried to improve existing ones. In the case of the flute every player of note left his mark: Briccialdi, Carte, Dorus, Radcliff, Rockstro, Pratten and many others. On the other hand, there was research into the nature of earlier instruments which had become classed as obsolete, speculation as to the nature of the old Cremona varnish, or what was an oboe da caccia or a viola bastada.

Interest was focused on improvements to instruments at the Great Exhibition of 1851; while there was a wonderful display of early instruments in the Loan Collection at the International Inventions Exhibition of 1885. This was commemorated in a beautifully illustrated book by Hipkins and Gibb. Other exhibitions followed, such as that organized by the Worshipful Company of Musicians in 1904 at the Fishmongers' Hall.

Then there were the great collectors, such as Engel, Mahillon, Donaldson, de Witt and Heyer. There were also the antiquarians, including the Bridges (Sir Frederick and Dr Joseph), Dr Southgate, Christopher Welch and others.

The recorder was not revived, however, through the activities of antiquarians, collectors, librarians and curators of museums, although their work helped to create an interest in early instruments and an admiration for their craftsmanship. Tribute must also be paid to the work of such musicians as Arkwright, Fuller-Maitland, Barclay Squire, Fellowes, Edward Naylor, Peter Warlock and Kennedy Scott, who all fostered an interest in Elizabethan music and helped to produce a climate in which the recorder could flourish.

Christopher Welch (1832-1915) introduced the recorder to the members of the Musical Association in 1898, with his paper on 'Literature relating to the Recorder'. He was followed in 1901 by Dr Joseph Cox Bridge, then organist at Chester Cathedral, whose

XXXI. Frans Bruggen

XXXII. Hans Coolsma

XXXIII. Friedrich von Huene.

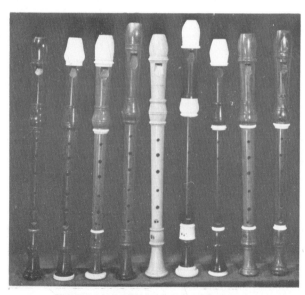

XXXIV. MODERN TREBLE RECORDERS
Left to right: Fehr, Kung, Dolmetsch, Dolmetsch low pitch,
Mollenhauer, Coolsma Bressan copy, Coolsma, Moeck
Rottenburgh model, von Huene.

subject was 'The Chester Recorders'. On this occasion the Gavotte by Henri le Jeune (from Mersenne, Fig. 13), a Duet for treble and bass recorders, and a Quartet composed for the occasion by the lecturer were played on this now-famous set of recorders, by the flautists, Radcliff and Finn, the Rev J.L. Bedford (who came from Chester and also played the pibcorn) and Dr J.C. Bridge. Many years later Dr Bridge told the writer that they did not properly understand the fingering of the instruments and treated them like whistles, covering the thumb-holes with stamp-paper! Nor did Dr Bridge at that time understand their pitch (which is the old chamber pitch, about ¾ tone flatter than normal), but imagined that 'six fingers' gave them F on the treble or C on the tenor. As a consequence, when Christopher Welch asked, in the discussion which followed, what their pitch was, Dr Bridge replied: 'They are pretty high—above the French, up to the Philharmonic pitch'.

Christopher Welch's second paper was on 'Hamlet and the Recorder' in 1902, and in 1904 a feature of the Fishmongers' Hall Exhibition was the series of lecture-recitals on different aspects of English Music. In the course of these John Finn (one of Dr Bridge's players) took as his subject 'The Recorder, Flute, Fife and Piccolo'. His lecture was afterwards published in a symposium entitled 'English Music'. In 1911 Welch's two Musical Association papers and some others were published under the title *Six Lectures on the Recorder and other Flutes in relation to Literature*.

Meanwhile Arnold Dolmetsch (1858-1940) had been pursuing his researches into the music for the viols, harpsichord and other early instruments; and also into their construction. He had stumbled on the viol music in the British Museum when looking for music for his viola d'amore, and that chance discovery had opened up a new vista of ensemble music for him. In 1903 he had acquired an old treble recorder, and spent a voyage to America studying its technique from one of those little eighteenth-century tutors, *The Compleat Flute-Master or the whole art of playing on ye Rechorder*. Doubtless he made rapid progress!

At the time, however, Dolmetsch went no further than to play little tunes on his lovely Bressan recorder at his lecture recitals, using it in 'broken consorts', the music for which still exists, and it was not until 1919 that chance forced his next step. By then the Dolmetsch family was established at Haslemere. The children were Cecile, Rudolph, Nathalie and Carl, and they all took part in the recitals with their parents. In the spring of 1919 they were returning to Haslemere after a concert, and while waiting to go onto the platform at Waterloo, Carl, who had charge of the bag containing the recorder, rested it on the platform. In the ensuing scramble for the train the bag was left behind and its loss not discovered until it was too late!

The misfortune, however, proved a challenge to Arnold Dolmetsch, who soon set about making a replacement—no mean task to undertake from his notes. Encouraged by the success of his first attempt, others were made for friends. In due course the lost recorder was seen in a curio shop opposite Waterloo Station by Mr F. G. Rendall of the British Museum, a fine amateur clarinettist, who bought it for 5/-. The instrument was generously returned to Arnold Dolmetsch, who showed his appreciation of Mr Rendall's kindness by giving him the first Dolmetsch recorder. —an historic instrument. The making of recorders had begun.

The treble recorder figured in the First Haslemere Festival in 1925. At the sixth concert, on August 29, the programme opened with five Spanish Popular Tunes for recorder, lute and viols. The same instruments were heard again on September 3, this time in *Watkins Ale* and *Munday's Joy,* but the recorders had really arrived when, on the following evening, Bach's Concerto in F for harpsichord, two recorders and strings was played. The recorder players were Rudolph Dolmetsch and Miles Tomalin. In the following year the quartet of recorders played, among other things, the Gavotte by Henri le Jeune, and some quintets in which Carl took part.

Among those who came to the first of these festivals were two Germans, Max Seiffert, the Handel scholar, and Peter Harlan, a guitarist and instrument maker. They at once saw the possibilities of these recorders for the performance of early music, and Harlan in particular realized what could be done with them in simple music-making. He bought a set of these instruments from Dolmetsch with the intention of copying them. Unfortunately he did not stop in Haslemere long enough to learn the correct fingering.

Back in Germany Harlan set about making recorders after the Dolmetsch pattern. One can imagine his problems. Like Dr Bridge's friends, he probably tried to play them 'like whistles' and expected the fourth note to sound in tune with just the first finger of the right hand, instead of the fork. It was not in tune; so he, quite naturally, thought Dolmetsch's ear rather inaccurate, and promptly made it in tune with that fingering. The result was a treble with a perfect B flat, but an impossibly sharp B natural—all right so long as you did not attempt to modulate to C major. This stupid mistake was the beginning of recorders 'with German fingering' which are still manufactured in large numbers and are to be found in shops all over the world, except, fortunately, in England.

But that was not all. Dolmetsch has adopted for his old instruments one of the eighteenth-century pitches, and they were a semitone flatter than normal. Nobody had warned Harlan of this, so, instead of making recorders in C and F at the low pitch, he thought he was making them in B and E normal pitch—the same thing, but a different name—and how do you play Handel's F major sonata on a treble in E? The keys of B and E had too many sharps in their signatures; so the next move was to make recorders in A and D instead. At least they would be able to team up with stringed instruments.

The movement towards the making and the playing of early instruments was not by any means confined to the Dolmetsch family in England. In Germany, Professor Gurlitt of Freiburg had established the Praetorius organ, while others were interested in the viols and the viola d'amore. In the case of the recorders Max Hüller, a director of Messrs G.H. Hüller, the wind instrument makers of Schöneck in Saxony, had already made some for Professor Dr Werner Danckert of the University of Jena in Thuringia. That was in 1924; and the recorders were played on the occasion of an educational music-week early in the following year.

Harlan and two of his friends played their new recorders in concerts all over Germany; and in 1927 Herr Emil Brauer ordered some recorders from Harlan, and these, together with some made by Hüller, formed the first complete set of recorders to be played in Germany. They were played for the first time in October 1928 at Essen-Ruhr, to provide interlude music for a play. The players were in costume, and the photograph shows Herr Brauer playing the bass recorder. (The other players were Herr Ellers, treble; Herr Wördehoff, descant; and Herr Testroet, tenor) (Plate XXX).

In 1929 Herr Brauer moved from Essen-Ruhr to Düsseldorf, where he collaborated with Herr F. J. Giesbert, an enthusiast for early music and a recorder player, in the formation of a society for both professionals and amateurs called *Die Sackpfeife,* whose main object was the playing of early music on the instruments for which it was written.

Since both Peter Harlan and Max Hüller had begun to make recorders, other wind instrument makers copied the idea, and soon the instrument was being played everywhere. But there was very little original music available. Musicians had not realized that much of Bach's and Handel's music required recorders, and there was a great danger of the lack of suitable music holding back the revival.

Back in England the story will, of necessity, become more and more autobiographical, and the writer will soon become tired of calling himself 'the writer', so he will change to 'I'!

By the time I left school in 1926, I had decided to make music my profession. My father was an organist and violinist, but I had always wanted to play a wind instrument, and had recently started to learn the flute. In 1926 I was awarded a flute scholarship at Trinity College of Music, London. I started there in the summer of 1927, studying the flute with Albert Fransella, and later with Robert Murchie. At the College I met Dr J.C. Bridge, who was Director of Studies, and he told me about the Chester recorders. I notice that my copy of Welch's book bears the date of my birthday in 1927. On October 2, 1928, I heard recorders played for the first time. The occasion was a recital at Oakfield Road Unitarian Church in Bristol, given by a group called 'the German Singers' who gave variety to their performance by using two Boehm flutes and a sestet of recorders. The players were:

Soprano recorder: Gertrud Zöllner
Tenor recorders: Fritz Relbach, H. Kümmerow
Alto recorders: Lotte Burdach, Marie Mattler
Bass recorder: Theodor Warner

In 1929 my father (organist of Bristol Cathedral) visited the Haslemere Festival. His report on the performances increased my interest in the recorder, and I went there myself the following summer. About this time I had my first recorder, bought from Oskar Dawson, who had been employed in the Dolmetsch workshops but had left to set up his own workshop in Haslemere, making recorders and clavichords. I also ordered a treble recorder from Bärenreiter, at Kassel in Germany. My Dawson treble, of course, had the traditional fingering and a very sweet tone. I used it at a number of concerts, the first being the Bristol Madrigal Society's Ladies Night in 1931, for which my father arranged Byrd's *Wolseys Wilde* and some other pieces for recorder, violin and viola. The next occasion of importance was the obbligato to Bach's *Höchster was ich habe* (Cantata 39) together with Dr Oldroyd and his lovely Kirkman harpsichord, at St Michael's East Croydon.

From the moment I first tried to play the recorder, I looked on it as complementary to my flute. The flute offered greater mechanical possibilities but demanded greater skill in certain directions: the recorder gave immediate response and seemed altogether more natural. Obviously many amateurs could play a recorder who would never get a note out of a flute! I was already visiting some schools to teach the flute and clarinet—why not start recorder ensembles as well, among the children whose parents could not afford those more costly instruments?

I soon found that there was no 'tutor' or 'Method for the Recorder' to be bought in England, apart from some little hand-written and lithographed booklets sold by the Dolmetsches—nothing, for instance, comparable to Otto Langey's Clarinet Tutor. There was a delightful *Blockflötenschule** by Robert Götz, and I had picked up a copy of *The Modern Music Master* (1731) for 10/- on a bookstall in Bristol, from which I found the eighteenth-century fingerings.

So I decided to fill the gap with a 'method' of my own. I had first to weigh up the merits of my Dawson recorder and *The Modern Music Master* on the one hand, with the Bärenreiter instrument (with its 'Harlan' fingering) and Robert Götz's *Blockflöten-schule* on the other. About this time a friend, one of the basses in the Bristol Madrigal Society, who had heard me play at their concert, lent and later gave me four beautiful old recorders which had been in his Yorkshire family for very many years. He was Mr C. E. Hoyland, and he told me that he had never heard them played. These instruments finally tipped the scale in favour of my

*P. J. Tonger, Cologne.

Dawson recorder. I found that I could play the Handel C major Sonata on Mr Hoyland's fine Bressan treble (the best of his four) and on my Dawson treble. There was, of course, a difference in pitch between them; but, fortunately, I had already dipped into Helmholtz and realized that the Bressan was at the eighteenth-century Kammer-Ton. But the Bärenreiter instrument was useless for this Handel sonata as all its B naturals were much too sharp. It was then that I coined the terms 'English fingering' and 'German fingering', and vowed not to import any more of the latter type of recorders.

In the autumn of 1931 I had completed the MS of *A Practical Method for the Recorder* and submitted it to Mr Hubert Foss at the Oxford University Press. The book was based on the treble recorder; but, instead of all the solo parts that one finds in the 'Langey' tutors, it was to include the nucleus of an ensemble repertory, with duets, trios and quintets which would include the other members of the family. Mr F. G. Rendall had enabled me to read at the British Museum before I had reached the statutory age of 21, and I had discovered there the quintets of Holborne as well as the duets of Paisible, the seventeenth-century 'Lessons' and a wealth of music by Daniel Purcell, Schickhard, Valentine, Loeillet, Mattheson, Pepusch and many others. Hubert Foss was interested in my MS; but as he was then actively preparing Gerald Hayes's books on early instruments for publication, he felt he must consult Arnold Dolmetsch. So Hubert Foss took my MS to Haslemere.

It must have been a difficult interview! Only a few months previously I had played the one-keyed *traversa* for Arnold Dolmetsch in Bach's *Peasant Cantata* at the 1931 Festival, and here I had had the nerve to write a book on a subject on which he and his family were the only possible authorities! After the first awkward moments, Hubert Foss persuaded Dolmetsch to let him bring out my book on condition I allowed my MS to be revised to accord with the Use of Haslemere, by Robert Donington who was then the secretary of the Dolmetsch Foundation. To this I agreed, against my better judgement, as I was anxious to see the book published. It was most unlikely that any other publisher would take the risk with an unknown author on an obscure subject and against the wishes of the other recorder players at Haslemere! But I say 'against my better judgement' as I think a book of that kind, thought out by one person, is better than a collaboration, unless the collaborators are persons who normally work and think to-gether. I felt so strongly about this and the resulting delays, that I prepared another book on different lines which I offered to Boosey and Hawkes. This was *A Concise Tutor for use in Schools.* As it happened, both came out in 1935!

Between 1931 and 1935 many things had happened to re-orient my work on the recorder. The *Practical Method* was directed mainly towards amateur ensembles, and included two of Anthony Holborne's quintets and other pieces with a bass, whereas *The Concise Tutor* catered primarily for the school instruments, the descant and treble.

In Germany any school child could buy a recorder for 5 Marks— a descant, but with German fingering. I was determined to do what I could to make similar instruments available in England but with English fingering. So, in 1934 I went with my friend, Emil Brauer, to the *Kasseler Musiktage.* There I was able to hear Gustav Scheck on the one-keyed *traversa* and recorder, August Wenzinger on the violoncello and viola da gamba and many other artists. Emil Brauer and I played a duet for recorder and *Dudelsack* (German bagpipe) in the *Gesellige Musik* (informal music-making) one afternoon. My recorder had to take the place of the *Schalmei* which would have normally accompanied the bagpipe, but which I could not play well enough. I was also able to see and compare the recorders made by Harlan, Herwig, Merzdorf, Moeck and Bärenreiter in the trade exhibition which was a feature of the festival. Through the good offices of Emil Brauer I secured the sole agency for the Herwig recorders in England. At that time Herwig was the only maker who was prepared to manufacture recorders with the English fingering, to my design, for the English market. I also met Hermann Moeck of Celle, for whom I later obtained a Dolmetsch treble recorder, as he wanted to study the differences involved in the two fingerings. Herwig also obtained a set of Dolmetsch recorders as models.

Back in England I imported a number of Herwig recorders for my pupils and others; but, when it came to supplying the larger wholesalers, I had not the capital to finance the customs duty as well as their quarterly accounts, and my rooms in Dulwich were not large enough to serve as a warehouse. Fortunately at this time I met

Mr Maynard Rushworth of the famous Liverpool firm, and told him of my business problems. The result was that he took over the Herwig agency and held it until the outbreak of World War II. This left me free to do more teaching, lecturing and editing.

Under the care of Mr Bickley of Rushworth's, the importing of Herwig recorders grew and a new line of cheaper descant recorders was produced, the 'Hamlin', which sold for 4/6 (=22½p).

When I first imagined recorders being played in schools, I thought of well-balanced consorts in public, grammar and high schools, and some in private schools—I did not think that 'council schools' would be interested. But an invitation from Dr Hooper, then of Bradford, made me change my ideas. In 1935 I had started my first recorder classes at Trinity College of Music, and not long afterwards (in 1937) Dr Hooper asked me to give a week's intensive course to about thirty Bradford school teachers. One of the 'students' on this course was Fred Fowler. Edmund Priestley took an interest in what we were doing, so I was pleased to see the result of their collaboration in *The School Recorder Book* which Arnold of Leeds published in 1937. Also in 1937 classes in 'Music-making through the Recorder' were started at the Mary Ward Settlement in London by Miss Freda Dinn; and these have now flourished for twenty-four years.

About this time the firm which had published my *Concise Tutor* started making some recorders. Unfortunately these instruments did nothing to enhance the firm's reputation. I do not think they realized how very difficult it is to make a good recorder that will sell at a low price. Herwig certainly had that know-how, and so did the firm of Adler which followed soon afterwards with instruments with English fingering for the English market.

The quality of the instruments available varied considerably, as well as the price. In this respect the price reflects what it costs to manufacture rather than how good (musically) the result is. In those days a Dolmetsch descant recorder cost five guineas, and that was a fair price for a fine instrument, individually made from a really hard wood. It only seemed expensive in comparison with mass-produced instruments, most of which were made of pear or maple. Of the latter, the 4/6 Hamlin descant was better value than many more expensive instruments from other makers because it was better tuned. A number of recorders were, and still are, made with so-called English fingering, whose only claim to such a title is the rather negative one, that they are not German fingered!

*   *   *

Apart from the trio which Arnold Dolmetsch wrote (1928) for descant, treble and tenor recorders, the first use of our instrument by a British composer was probably by Robin Milford (if we except the little pieces written by Dr Bridge and one of the Galpins for private use and to illustrate lectures). Milford introduced an interlude for recorder and harpsichord into his Oratorio *A Prophet in the Land* which was performed at a Three Choirs Festival in 1930. The Oratorio has not, as far as I know, been revived; but in 1958 Robin Milford rescued this interlude from oblivion and wrote two more pieces to go with it and form his 'Three Airs' for treble recorder and harpsichord. The second Air is the original one.

In the spring of 1932 a little festival of music was held at a school in Plön, and Paul Hindemith provided all the music for the young musicians taking part. *The Plöner Musiktag*, as this musical field day was called, started with a piece for trumpets and trombones. Then there was a cantata in which all could take part, while the *Abendkonzert* consisted of smaller items for flute, clarinet and strings and a *Trio für Blockflöten* which was played by Hindemith himself with two friends. The score is marked '*einzeln oder chorisch besetzt*' so we have the composer's authority for treating it either as chamber music or orchestrally with doubled parts. It was written for recorders in A and D, and this meant that it was rarely played in England, until in 1952 Hindemith authorized Dr Walter Bergmann to make a new edition for C and F recorders. This has given it a firm place in the repertory.

By about 1933 the recorder (with German fingering) was well established in Germany. The movements for encouraging music in the home and among young people were closely linked with the revival of pre-classical music and of viols, recorders and harpsichords. Giesbert was bringing out early music in his *Blätter der Sackpfeife* (published by Adolph Nagel, Hannover), and there was another series entitled *Musica Practica* which was edited by R. Heyden and W. Twittenhoff (Nagel). *Der Blockflöten-Spiegel* (The Recorder Mirror) was a monthly devoted to early music and the recorder in particular. It was published by Hermann Moeck of

Celle and included a music supplement. This magazine started in 1931 under the editorship of Giesbert but after four years its supplement had assumed more importance and became *Die Zeitschrift für Spielmusik*, while the magazine ceased publication. *Der Blockflöten-Spiegel* and *Die Zeitschrift für Spielmusik* (which continues to this day) were both published by Moeck of Celle. A third force behind this movement, or grouping of movements, was the Bärenreiter Verlag of Kassel. This firm organized the *Arbeitskreis für Hausmusik* and the *Kasseler Musiktage* and published *Die Zeitschrift für Hausmusik* as the monthly journal of the Arbeitskreis.

In this way the recorder movement was in good hands in Germany, linked with the revival of other early instruments and with a musical do-it-yourself—*Hausmusik*. More and more music was being made available, but the difference of fingering separated the German from the English movements. Perhaps it was as well, for the next event was the XI Olympic Games in Berlin, which were opened with a demonstration of 'Olympic Youth' in which 6,000 children, boys and girls, gave a gymnastic display to the music of Carl Orff, played by the Youth Orchestra of the Munich *Güntherschule* under Gunild Keetman, in which recorders figured prominently with all kinds of percussion instruments! The recorder was acquiring political associations and soon became the instrument of the Hitler Youth, for which all kinds of marches, including the *Horst Wessel-Lied*, were to be arranged.

In England the Haslemere Festivals were established as annual events, and through them the recorder developed as an instrument. It is interesting to follow some of those improvements which were 'invented' in the Dolmetsch workshops, such as 'double holes' and the sopranino recorder. In 1927 Carl Dolmetsch had taken part in a performance of Purcell's *Dioclesian* when the bass part of the Chaconne had been played on a bass recorder by Miss Margaret Donington. The part required a low A flat but no A natural; so what was simpler than to insert a ring into the A hole to reduce its size and flatten the note a semitone. This experiment was successful and gave Carl the idea of double holes for the low F sharp and G sharp of the treble recorder and for the corresponding notes of the other instruments. He did not at the time know about the Chester recorders or that the idea had already been suggested by

Hotteterre. Somewhat similar was the 'invention' of the sopranino, before its place in *Acis and Galatea* was realized, or old examples seen. It used to be said, jokingly, of Arnold Dolmetsch that if he went on long enough making harpsichords, he would invent the piano! Carl seemed to follow in his father's footsteps!

1935 saw the start of a new quarterly, *The Amateur Musician*, edited and published by a Miss Elizabeth Voss. When I wrote an article on *The Recorder or English Flute* for the third issue I did not know that I should become co-editor by No. 8, and marry my co-editor before No. 15, but that is how it happened! In the fifteenth issue of this magazine there was an article on *The Recorder—Its tone, as revealed by composers of the seventeenth and eighteenth centuries* by C. M. Champion. I first met Max Champion and his wife, Stephanie, about 1933. Max and I were both flautists and former pupils of Albert Fransella, Stephanie was a viola player and pianist and not so enthusiastic about recorders at first. Max and I spent many a lunch hour together discussing Hotteterre or Handel, and when Stephanie had been convinced that recorders could be played in tune, and had taken up the tenor as well as the treble, we formed a trio to give performances of recorder music.

Some time in 1937 there were a number of little recorder music books in the window of Schott and Co in Great Marlborough Street: *Schöne Musikanten, spielet auf, Erstes Zusammenspiel* (now better known in England as Giesbert's *First Ensemble*) and a number of others. I looked at them, but did not buy—when asked why, I said that at 1/- each they were too expensive, but I thought they ought to sell well at 6d! The result was an interview with Max Steffens, the firm's managing director, as a result of which I joined the staff of Schott's. Not only were the little books reduced to 6d, but many more followed, and in 1938 I produced the first comparable booklets in England: *Twelve National Airs,* and *Twelve Christmas Carols.* Before long Schott's also held the British Empire agencies for Nagel, Bärenreiter, Moeck and Vieweg, the chief publishers of recorder music on the Continent; they also began to stock the Herwig recorders, so that the shop in Great Marlborough Street became truly the 'Centre for Recorder Players'.

Then in October, 1937, The Society of Recorder Players was founded. I had known the activities in similar spheres of The

Pipers' Guild and of The London Flute Society (I had been its last conductor before it disbanded), and I felt that there was a genuine need for a society to bring together recorder players. Plans were discussed with Max and Stephanie Champion and I was preparing lists of all the recorder players I had met through my work at Schott's and through my teaching at Trinity College. Then the Champions heard that Carl Dolmetsch was planning a similar society. We could very easily have formed two separate and rival societies, but it was entirely due to the Champions' influence and tact that one society was formed, with Stephanie as Hon. Secretary, Max as Chairman, and with Carl and me as Musical Directors under the Presidency of Arnold Dolmetsch. The meetings were held in London for a long time at the Hall of the Art Workers' Guild. When we played together—a group of about 30 to 40—it used to take about ten minutes to get most of us in tune; but our patience was worthwhile as the standard of performance by the average members of the society has risen beyond all our dreams, and when the London Branch of the Society now sits down to play on a Saturday afternoon, the result is worth hearing.

Max Steffens was present at some of our early discussions; and recorder players owe much to his benign influence, and for his interest in keeping the Society's publications alive during the war years.

One of my pupils, Mr Manuel Jacobs, was a devotee of contemporary music as well as the recorder. He was not at all satisfied with the *Spielmusik* that was coming out of Germany, and felt, like many others, that something should be done about it. He was a very determined young man, who would not take 'no' for an answer; and the result of his efforts was the composition of a series of Sonatinas for treble recorder and piano by some of the most talented young composers of the time—Stanley Bate, Lennox Berkeley, Christian Darnton, Peggy Glanville-Hicks, Eve Kisch, Walter Leigh, Peter Pope, Alan Rawsthorne and Franz Reizenstein.

At a meeting of the London Contemporary Music Centre on June 17, 1939, Carl Dolmetsch and I were invited to play two each of these new works. Carl played the Berkeley and Bate, while I chose the Darnton and Pope. Three members of the Dolmetsch family played the Hindemith Trio on this occasion. The Rawsthorne, Darnton and Kisch Sonatinas were withdrawn by their respective composers, but all the others were in due course published.

On February 1, 1939, Carl Dolmetsch and Joseph Saxby gave their first Wigmore Hall recital. In the first issue of *The Recorder News*, Carl wrote: 'One of my aims will be to demonstrate the possibilities of the recorder as a virtuoso instrument on a par with the already accepted violin, flute or pianoforte, and to present masterpieces of music which form part of its literature.' These Wigmore recitals became annual events. At the first Carl played a composition of his own designed to let the recorder show its paces. The next year he had the Lennox Berkeley Sonatina; and when he had introduced the Bate and some others, he commissioned other composers, including Herbert Murrill, Gordon Jacob, Martin Shaw, York Bowen, Cyril Scott, Edmund Rubbra and many more, and introduced works by other contemporary composers such as Arnold Cooke, Antony Hopkins and Georges Migot.

In the same year I was invited by Mr Fairfax Jones, the Secretary of the Federation of British Music Competition Festivals, to direct the first Summer School for Recorder Players, as a part of one of the Downe House Summer Schools which were held each year near Newbury. About a dozen 'students' of all ages attended this week which proved to be the first of twenty-two.

With the outbreak of World War II there were no more cheap recorders from Germany, nor music; so my first job was to produce a substitute here. Wood was out of the question, so we tried cellulose acetate, and the first of the little black Schott Descant recorders was born. These instruments produced a pleasant tone, but the material was liable to change its shape alarmingly if left in the sun or near a fire, so we had to change to bakelite as a more serviceable material, even though the tone was inclined to be harsh.

These cheap recorders were at first, quite understandably, viewed with suspicion by the Dolmetsches, but they soon came to appreciate their usefulness and in due course, after the war admirable plastic recorders were also made by Arnold Dolmetsch Ltd.

Far from stopping the spread of the recorder, the war and its new conditions only served to increase the demand for music and instruments. Schools had been evacuated from the larger cities to country districts, and often there were no pianos to lead the singing. Recorders were sent for. In February, 1940, Dr Hooper wrote to tell me of the progress of recorder playing in the Bradford schools, and how in one instance the recorder class turned up even though their school was closed. Their music had to go on!

My Trinity College of Music recorder classes had to close, together with other evening activities, until after the war. But there were courses in the country and broadcasts. So much interest was aroused through one broadcast that I started a four-page News Letter, which ran for six issues in 1940, and helped to keep recorder players in touch with events until the air raids on London stopped production. There was another broadcast early in 1941 (with the Champions), in a series entitled 'Music-Makers' Half-Hour', not long after our Fleet Street flat was destroyed, when I played on my recorders which had been miraculously rescued from the debris. A month later I was in the army and, apart from a week on leave at Downe House and two short broadcasts to the troops in India, put away my recorders until 1946.

World War II was different from all previous wars in the way music was encouraged, not only for the Forces but among civilians. Sir Walford Davies had the idea of C.E.M.A. (the Council for the Encouragement of Music and the Arts in Wartime) before his death in 1941, and much excellent work was done by his 'Travellers in Music' and under its auspices. Naturally there were many problems. On the one hand there were shortages of music and instruments: on the other, growing demands for such supplies as there were. Max and Stephanie Champion formed a little recorder group at their A.R.P. post, while the Dolmetsch workshops were making parts for aeroplanes. But the man who did most to keep the recorder and its music alive at this time was Dr Walter Bergmann, through the classes which he started for recorder players at Morley College in London, and through his work at Schott's where he took over my job.

8

THE RECORDER TODAY

One of the phenomena of our time is the sustained popularity and use of the recorder in so many different fields. Here, in England, it is widely used in primary schools—some might say misused, as the teaching is not always in the hands of experts. The use of the recorder in education is basically right, as it provides instrumental training in melody after rhythm has been taught through percussion instruments. For far too long singing had been the only form of music cultivated in school and it was high time a due balance between the instrumental and vocal was restored.

Recorder playing trains ears, eyes and fingers. Ears to check intonation, eyes to read music and fingers ready to try other instruments later on. It also trains children in elementary ensemble. Children who play the recorder are not just the pawns in an education project but heirs to a tradition, learning a technique which will be useful to them if later they wish to pursue it further, or should they want to take up some other wind instrument. This could not, for instance, be claimed for the mouth organ.

From their primary schools children go on to some form of secondary education, and here the secondary modern school offers the best opportunities for the recorder group, though it is known to flourish also in some grammar and technical schools. Some primary school teachers deplore the fact that when their children move on there are not enough opportunities for recorder playing in their secondary schools; though efforts are often made to provide the desired continuity.

Some of the results of all this recorder playing and teaching are seen in Music Festivals throughout the country. There are recorder classes in many teacher-training colleges, but the standard of teaching is not yet high owing to the shortage of instructors who are expert in this as well as in so many other fields. To help raise the standard of teaching the Society of Recorder Players began in 1948 to organize 'The Recorder in Education' Summer Schools. At these the music comes first and the recorder is treated as a means of making music rather than as an 'educational' weapon.

For many years Trinity College of Music was the only one of the music colleges in London to place the recorder on a footing equal to that accorded to other subjects. All first-year students taking the graduate course there attend classes in recorder playing, while any student who wishes can study the recorder up to diploma standard, and in fact take the L.T.C.L. diploma either as teacher or performer. The diploma itself is not an isolated examination, as there is a graded series of pupils' examinations leading to it, one of which is accepted by some university examining boards for G.C.E. purposes. Now, however, the recorder is taught at the Royal College of Music, The Royal Academy of Music, The Guildhall School of Music, The London College of Music, the Birmingham Music School and the Royal Northern College of Music, and the number of recorder diplomas has been multiplied.

The Society of Recorder Players is largely responsible for the progress of the recorder in this country. With the gradual return to normality after World War II, the time came for a reorganization of the Society. It had lost its President by the death on February 28, 1940, of Arnold Dolmetsch, and Mr and Mrs Champion felt that the time had come for others to contribute something to the movement, so they resigned their offices. The Society, therefore, was reconstituted on a new and wider basis. Dr Percy Scholes became the new President. The work of Freda Dinn and Dr Walter Bergmann was recognized by making them joint Musical Directors with Carl Dolmetsch, while I became the Society's Chairman. Apart from changes of Secretary and President, the same team continued for many years. Dr Benjamin Britten, C.H., accepted the Society's Presidency after the death in 1958 of Dr Percy Scholes. In 1972 I resigned the Chairmanship of the S.R.P. to be succeeded by Mr Theo Wyatt.

The long and continued service of the Society's officers meant much to the recorder movement in Great Britain. Each could contribute something special and personal to the unity and progress of the Society and the movement as a whole. Our President as a composer uses recorders as naturally as any other instruments on his palette, exploring original effects, as in the storm music and cooing of the dove in *Noye's Fludde,* the use of sopraninos in *A Midsummer Night's Dream,* the lively impressions of his *Alpine Suite* and the gaiety of his Scherzo for recorder quartet. Together with Imogen Holst, Dr Britten directed the policy of Messrs

Boosey and Hawkes's publications for recorders.

Dr Carl Dolmetsch, C.B.E., is a soloist, recorder maker and teacher of international reputation. With Joseph Saxby, his tours to New Zealand and the United States, as well as to many European countries and at home, have done much to show that the recorder is by no means confined to playing little folk songs. Together with his pupil, Layton Ring (a New Zealander), he is responsible for the English recorder publications of Universal Edition.

Freda Dinn, through her long association as lecturer with the Froebel Educational Institute at Roehampton, did much to further the cause of the recorder in educational circles. For a time the Society had a Junior Section under her leadership and this was only closed when it became clear that educational authorities would be doing for the children most of the things which this section had started. Dr Walter Bergmann's flair for the organization of music-making and concerts has been of the greatest value to the Society, while his editions published by Schott's combine scholarship, wit and musicianship. When Michael Tippett (one of the Society's Vice-Presidents) resigned his Directorship of the Music at Morley College, Dr Bergmann left also and for a time made the Mary Ward Settlement a centre for his musical activities. My own contribution has been in the educational field as professor for the recorder at Trinity College of Music, directing the Summer School for Recorder Players at Downe House, and later the Anglo-French and Anglo-German courses, bringing the experience of organizing such courses to the 'Recorder in Education' Summer School, besides editing music and designing recorders for mass production.

The framework of the Society was changed where conditions demanded. In the beginning the Society used to meet in London although there were members scattered throughout the country and abroad. Now London is regarded as a branch, and new branches are formed wherever a large enough group exists. The first of these branches were at Birmingham and Bristol. Manchester followed soon afterwards and was later joined by Liverpool and Newcastle. At present there are, altogether, some two dozen branches in the British Isles.

The Society of Recorder Players' concern for raising the standard of playing (and teaching) was reflected in the early institution of a teacher's test. Before World War II there had been fifteen successful candidates and since the war further certificates were awarded. The aim of these tests was to form a panel of teachers who could be recommended when inquiries came.

When the Society was founded in 1937 relatively little music for recorder ensembles was published in this country and the Society undertook to bring out an edition for its members. These publications were discontinued in 1956 as it was no longer necessary for the Society to compete against the normal publishers, who were by then constantly providing new music of all kinds. The last two numbers of this series, Nos. 20 and 21, were noteworthy publications: *Four Inventions* for descant and treble recorders by Michael Tippett and a Suite for two trebles and tenor by Peter Racine Fricker. To the Oxford University Press and Boosey and Hawkes must go the credit for providing the first British editions of recorder music in the present revival. Then came Schott's, Paxton (music for recorders to go with percussion band), Joseph Williams and Curwen. Schott's have maintained their lead ever since but have been re-joined by O.U.P. and Boosey. Universal Edition, Mills Music, Ricordi and Lengnick have added their quota, while many continental publishers are represented by Novello's and Hinrichsen. The difficulty is not to find recorder music but to select from the quantity that is available.

Since this book was first published in 1962 many London music publishers have disappeared from the scene—either suffered amalgamation with others or moved out of London; but we can still look for significant works that have been published since 1945. Starting with Boosey and Hawkes, there are the works by Benjamin Britten which I have already mentioned and a delightful duet for two trebles by Lennox Berkeley. The Oxford University Press offers Herbert Murrill's Sonata, Robin Milford's *Three Airs* and a *Christmas Pastorale,* and Gordon Jacob's *Suite* for recorder and strings or piano. There is a quantity of music for school use, but among the ensemble pieces Anthony Baines has arranged some excellent quintets from Matthew Locke's pieces for the Royal Sackbuts and Cornetts, and there are some quintets by Anthony Holborne salvaged from *A Practical Method.* Universal Edition's *Il Flauto Dolce* series offers a number of good things from the eighteenth century and earlier, from which I should select the *Suite* by Nichola Matteis—a brilliant solo for descant recorder. But one of the most charming items is Herbert Murrill's *For my Friends*—a little piece written for two recorders and harpsichord and dedicated to Carl Dolmetsch's two daughters. Other modern works are Dr Hans Gal's *Quartettino* and some pieces by Peter Crossley-Holland.

Some composers are always associated with a particular publisher and we must look for Malcolm Arnold's Sonatina at Patterson's and Edmund Rubbra's music at Lengnick's. Rubbra's *Meditazioni sopra Coeurs Desolées* for recorder and harpsichord or piano is, in my opinion, one of the finest recorder pieces of the present century. He has also written a Sonatina for recorder and harpsichord, a piece for recorder, strings and harpsichord, another with soprano voice, a recorder quartet, etc.

There are some important contemporary works for recorder in Schott's catalogue. Francis Baines's masterly Quartet for two trebles and two tenors and his effective (and easier) Fantasia for three descants and three trebles are first in importance; and are closely followed by the Hindemith Trio, suites for three recorders by Müller-Hartmann and Timothy Moore and for four recorders by John Graves and Gaston Saux. Among the solo pieces pride of place goes to Antony Hopkins's brilliant *Suite* for descant recorder and piano.

On the lighter side mention must be made of Walter Bergmann's arrangements for recorders and piano of some dances from the 'Apted Book' and Brian Bonsor's *Rumba* and *Beguine*. The craftsmanship of these pieces is admirable. Robert Salkeld excels as a teacher and his *First Concert Pieces* have lightened the tasks of many an instructor and his class.

So much recorder playing could not fail to produce some outstanding players. Stanley Taylor (1902-1972) formed a trio with his two sons—both professional flautists—and one of them, Richard Taylor, partnered Carl Dolmetsch in a performance of Brandenburg IV at an Albert Hall Promenade Concert in 1956. Philip Rodgers of Sheffield received the dedication of three effective modern solo works: the sonatinas of Malcolm Arnold and Colin Hand and Dr Arnold Cooke's Concerto for recorder and strings. John Sothcott has a facile technique, and Marylin Wailes has explored much early music with her group. David Munrow has done much to popularize the recorder and the music of the Renaissance.

Others who are often before the public include Michael Arno, Michael Muskett, Alan Davis (Birmingham), Edgar Gordon and Christopher Ball. There is a third generation of the Dolmetsches following the family tradition. Richard, the youngest, died tragically in 1966, but the twins, Jeanne and Marguerite, take part in the Haslemere Festivals and other concerts.

The Anglo-French Recorder Courses and opportunities to study abroad have broken down some national and language barriers with the result that some of our most talented players live and work abroad: Anita Davies (Amsterdam), Jennifer Kliphuis (née Brook–Utrecht), Beverly Barbey (née Smith–Beauvais) and Judith Vaumoron (née Gibbons–Amsterdam, Milan and Paris until her death in 1973).

Festivals organized on a national scale by the S.R.P. have brought to the fore some outstanding young players, among them: Evelyn Nallen, Catherine Marwood, and Ross Winters. Ross, taught first by his father Leslie Winters, read music at Oxford and finished his training in Amsterdam.

In Belgium the Pro Musica Antiqua group under Safford Cape must have been one of the first to present programmes of renaissance music, and the playing of Henri Koenig its recorder player was much admired. Since then such activities in Belgium have been overshadowed by those in Holland, but a revival is due. The first International Recorder Festival was held at Bruges in 1972 and will take place every three years (the second in 1975) as part of the Festival van Vlaanderen.

My friend Kurt Ziener told me that the recorder movement in Denmark started about 1930, when some young musicians brought the instruments home from Germany. After a tour by Fritz Jöde, in 1932, the first *Folkemusikskole* was established with recorder playing in the curriculum. Up to 1945 the recorder was played by amateurs in private groups; but after the war it began to be used in schools.

As many of those trying to teach the recorder had very little knowledge of the instrument the *Studiekredsen for Blokfljtelaereve* (study circle for recorder teachers) was formed as a section of *Musikpaedagogisk Forening* (the Society of authorized teachers of music), and there have been summer courses at which the classes have been taken by leading teachers from Germany such as Monkemeyer, Dr Hildemarie Peter and Elly Rohr, and the late Conrad Fehr from Switzerland. In 1957 the Danish Ministry of Education authorized a *Musikpaedagogisk Eksamen* (examination for teachers) in recorder, equivalent to that for other instruments. A leading teacher and performer is Irmgard Knopf Mathiesen who leads the recorder group, Concentus Musicus.

In Norway and Sweden the influence has been mainly German, with German-fingered instruments in the schools, but with good players as teachers, such as Kari Johnsen (Minde, Norway) the situation must improve. The two little recorder-like instruments shown on Plate II, Nos. 1 and 2, both come from Norway. No. 1 has six holes, like a penny whistle, while No. 2 is constructed like a recorder with German fingering, but neither is as well tuned as the average school recorder.

If the recorder was first revived as an instrument for the performance of early music in England, to Germany must go the honour of being the home of the more popular use of the instrument. But, although the recorder figures prominently in the work of the folk-music schools there are also many who respect it as the right instrument for the music of Bach, Handel and Telemann, and we owe to the German publishers a large proportion of the new editions of music from the eighteenth-century and earlier, some modern works of importance and some that are representative of the *avant-garde*.

While the recorder is represented by a few items in the catalogues of Peters and Breitkopf and Härtel (including *avant-garde* works by Jurg Baur); such firms as Nagel, Moeck and Bärenreiter may be said to have grown up with the recorder movement and to share with the old-established house of B. Schotts Söhne of Mainz most of the important publications for the recorder.

A very large proportion of these are editions of eighteenth-century sonatas. Of the contemporary works it is difficult to separate the *Spielmusik* and easy pieces for beginners from the real music. Some attractive pieces have come from the pens of such composers as Alfred von Beckerath, Cesar Bresgen, Harald Genzmer, and Gerhard Wohlgemuth and there are important works by Karl Marx of Stuttgart, and Gerhard Maasz and Felicitas Kukuck, both of Hamburg.

Most of the leading players and teachers of Germany acknowledge Professor Gustav Scheck as their teacher and musical leader. As a performer he is equally at home with the modern flute, the eighteenth-century traversa and the recorder. Born in 1901 at Munich, he came under the influence of Professor Gurlitt at Freiburg when a student at the university there, and his interest in early music was kindled. In the 1930s he was teaching at the *Hochschule für Musik* in Berlin, and wrote a masterly chapter on the recorder, which he called *Die Langsflöte*, in Dr Müller-Blattau's *Hohe Schule der Musik*. In this he covered the instrument's early history and technique; but, in those days, he was using the German fingering which, like other leading players, he has now abandoned. As a performer he has toured widely, visiting India, Japan, Turkey and Brazil, as well as the more usual centres of music; and, after the war, founded the *Staatliche Hochschule für Musik* at Freiburg, which he directed until his retirement. Professor Scheck uses a beautiful ivory recorder made by the late Hans Conrad Fehr of Zürich who was one of his pupils.

Ferdinand Conrad is well known to English recorder players through his articles on ornamentation which appeared in *The Recorder News* and were reprinted in *The Recorder and Music Magazine,* and through his master classes and teaching at courses. He was a pupil of Gustav Scheck in Berlin (also of Emil Prill, the flautist), and teaches at the *Niedersächsische Hochschule für Musik und Theater* in Hanover. He has recorded for the Archiv series of *Deutsche Gramophon* and *Pelikan* (Zürich).

A pupil of Herr Conrad, Ingetraud Drescher, taught the recorder at the *Musikakademie* in Kassel; and there are many other teachers holding similar positions in Heidelberg, Mannheim and Brunswick. Nikolaus Delius of Karlsruhe was a pupil of Gustav Scheck and also teaches at Freiburg.

In Berlin there are Dr. Hildemarie Peter (Frau Streich) whose thesis on *The Recorder—its traditions and its tasks* and edition of the *Fontegara* of Ganassi are well known; Thea von Sparr and Herr Rudolf Barthel. Herr Barthel (who has visited England with his class) has revived the methods of Mersenne by organizing his players as an orchestra in which the higher and lower groups of instruments can be treated like the 4' and 8' registers of an organ. He balances his players in the following proportion:

(1)	1 Sopranino	(2)	7 Tenors
(4)	8 Descants	(3)	5 Basses
(3)	8 Trebles	(1)	4 Great Basses

using a band of 33 players. The figures in brackets are for a more modest band of 14. With such groups various arrangements can be adopted. The music can be arranged in either two or three 'tiers'. In a two-tiered arrangement, some trebles, some tenors, basses and great basses can form the lower register, with the sopranino, descants, and the rest of the trebles and tenors doubling at the octave: or, in a three-tiered setting, a central group of descants, trebles and tenors can be doubled at the octave either above or below, or both. Herr Barthel recommends the following arrangement of his forces:

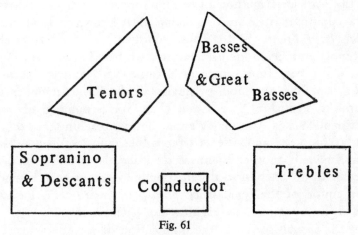

Fig. 61

Music for such an orchestra, original works as well as arrangements, is published by Sirius-Verlag of Berlin. The Haiger Blockflötenkreis, directed by Herr Gunter Neumann, is a similar orchestra which has often combined with English players in Anglo-German Summer Schools.

Recorders fit naturally into the scheme of the *Schulwerk* or 'Music for Children' of Carl Orff and Gunild Keetman. Most of the instruments are tuned percussion; glockenspiels, metallophones and xylophones; but the teacher's manual, translated by Doreen Hall of Toronto, says of the recorder:
'It is essential that the teacher be able to play and improvise freely on the recorder whether the children are doing rhythmic

body movements or basic ostinati on the instruments. The soft, reedy tone blends well with the whole ensemble and has a unique effect when used as a solo instrument.'

In Austria much of the pioneer work was done by Kurt Pitsch (Dipl. Ing.) of Linz who was largely responsible for the organization of summer courses for recorder players in Salzburg and Innsbruck. These attracted players from other countries including parties from England led by Dr Bergmann and Elli McMullen. These courses were continued under the direction of Rudolf Schwarz, while Herr Pitsch turned his attention to music-making at Schloss Burgeis in North Italy, amongst the German-speaking community there. In Vienna Professor Ulrich Staeps taught the recorder at the *Hochschule* where he also incorporated the use of the instrument into the Carl Orff method of teaching music. Professor Staeps is also a composer of some originality. Best known in England are his *Sieben Flötentänze* for four recorders (descant, two trebles and tenor) and *Reihe kleiner Duette* (two trebles); but he has also published a very fine Sonata in E flat (1951) and a *Sonate im alten Stil* besides a number of smaller works. Rene Clemencic was a pupil of Professor Staeps and then, for a number of years, director of Musica Antiqua, Vienna. Besides teaching the recorder he is a composer and directs Drama Musicum of Vienna. Hans-Maria Kneihs is another Viennese recorder player and cellist, and leader of the Wiener Blockflötenensemble, a group which specialises in music of the renaissance played on instruments based on those in the Kunsthistorisches Museum, Vienna.

Austria is well served in the publication of recorder music, for besides the Austrian half of Universal Edition there are Doblinger, Haslinger and Stanberg in Vienna, and Heinrich Müller at Salzburg.

Switzerland makes good use of the recorders in schools, and supports two of the finest recorder makers. Conrad Fehr has already been mentioned as a pupil of Gustav Scheck, Fehr himself died in 1958, but his workshops in Zürich are still active, carrying on the work he started so well. The recorders of Küng of Schaffhausen are noted for their evenness of tone and true intonation. Another pupil of Gustav Scheck, Hans-Martin Linde, is Switzerland's best-known recorder player, teacher and composer. Michel Piguet, better known for his playing on the baroque oboe, also plays the recorder.

In France the recorder movement did not at first make the rapid progress that has been reported so far from other European countries, and the reasons were many. We have already seen how the baroque recorder was probably born at la Couture-Boussey in the workshop of one of the Hotteterres. The French flageolet survived right into the nineteenth century, in the fashionable quadrille bands, and few musicians probably spared a thought for flûtes à bec when regarding the heritage of their music. When I was looking at the wonderful recorders in the private collection of Madame Thibault de Chambure, I came across a tenor, obviously copied from an old one, on the butterfly key of which I read the following: 'P. R. Souvenir de Couture, 1875', and on the head of this very fine instrument: 'J. B. Martin à son ami Paul Roche'. Here was an example of a maker's loving care for the instrument and skill in its manufacture. But an isolated instrument does not constitute a revival!

In the 1930s the bamboo pipe movement had a small following in France, and some charming pieces for these instruments were contributed by leading composers, such as Milhaud, Roussel and Auric, to 'Pipeaux 1934'. Some of these little pieces can be played effectively on the recorder.

The recorder movement in France has not been helped by the confusion in people's minds between these 'pipeaux', all kinds of six-holed whistles and the true recorder. Some little books for *flûtes douces* were brought out about 1935, but it is clear that the *flûte douce* does not always mean recorder. For instance, there is a *Méthode* by A. Ravizé, published by Durand, for '*Flûte douce, pipeau et flageolet*' from which we can see that a six-holed whistle and not a recorder is intended. Instruction is further confused when we look further and find that it is based on 'six-fingers C' instead of the 'six-fingers D' customary for such instruments. All this points to muddled thinking and amateurishness.

However, there are brighter spots in the publications of Aug. Zurfluh and Max Eschig (the Paris Schott). The *Méthode complète de Flûte à Bec (ou flûte douce)* by Roger Cotte breathes the air of Hotteterre and is one of the best instruction books in any language. But the person who is doing most for the movement in France is Jean Henry whose *Initiation Instrumentale par la Flûte à Bec* is probably the most detailed method, and one which is designed to fit the French educational system. The flautists Michel Dubost and Pierre Paubon both play the *flûte à bec,* and Georges Migot, who was Conservateur of the Museum of instruments at the Paris Conservatoire, has composed for the recorders. Another composer for the instrument was Gaston Saux whose Trio *Pour une Eglogue Virgilienne* and two Quartets have been published. Michel Sanvoisin, a pupil of Jean Henry, has emerged as a soloist and editor of recorder music published by Heugel.

The greatest contribution during the last twelve years has been that of Holland. After World War II Joannes Collette and Kees Otten emerged as the leading teachers and performers—Collette in the east round Nijmegen, Arnhem and Maastricht; Kees Otten to the west in Amsterdam and Rotterdam. They collaborated in an ensemble specializing in music before 1600, *Muziekkring Obrecht.* Collette wrote an excellent method, *Leidraad tot het Spel op de Alt-Blokfluit* (published by C. W. H. Snoek, Rotterdam), a book of *Acht Melodische Studien* (Ixijzet, Amsterdam) and a book of studies for descant recorder (Universal). Kees Otten was a frequent broadcaster and a number of pieces were written for him by Henk Badings and others. He also used his recorder in jazz (he had his own band and played clarinet) and achieved a remarkable *glissando* effect.

In amateur circles Gerrit Vellekoop, the editor of *Huismuziek,* has led the revival of the *Blokfluit* or *Handfluyt* as it used to be called. He has also placed recorder players in his debt as editor of van Eyck's *Der Fluyten Lust-Hof.*

In the 1960s a pupil of Kees Otten, Frans Brüggen, emerged as an outstanding recorder player, teacher and musicologist—a soloist of world stature with a formidable technique and the personality to hold an audience spellbound. Collaborating with the Utrecht recorder maker, Hans Coolsma, Brüggen guided the production of recorders of high quality from about 1962 onwards. His recordings of the Handel and Telemann recorder sonatas (Telefunken) established his mastery as well as the quality of Coolsma's recorders. For these recordings Brüggen also had the collaboration of Gustav Leonhardt, the eminent Dutch harpsichordist who was leading the movement towards authenticity in instruments as well as interpretation—the two are inseparable—and there began an important partnership. In 1965/66 I lent

Brüggen my Bressan treble recorder for some recordings and concerts and he had a copy of it made by Martin Skovroneck of Bremen. This in turn led to Hans Coolsma making a series of 100 copies of this instrument in 1966/68. These were not exact copies as Coolsma raised the pitch about ¼ tone to a′ =415, a semitone below the modern standard a′ =440, the wood was grenadilla instead of the old box, and he gave them double holes like the Chester Bressan. But he copied the important double curvature of the narrow wind-way and undercut fingerholes. Brüggen used the original Bressan and a number of other recorders from museums and private collections for a series of recordings of original instruments.

All this gave encouragement to the movement towards authenticity in the performance of baroque music. Other makers copied the Bressan and other baroque recorders: Friedrich von Huene (U.S.A.), Fred Morgan (Australia), Klaus Scheele (Germany), Andreas Glatt (Belgium) are a few examples. These are individual craftsmen making a limited number of instruments for soloists— generally with long waiting lists. To cater for the large number of players, students and amateurs, who also needed recorders with narrow curved wind-ways that would give the authentic baroque tone quality, von Huene designed the Rottenburgh series for production by the Moeck workshops at Celle, taking as his model instruments by J. H. Rottenburgh in the museum of the Brussels Conservatoire. So great is the interest in Holland in the voicing of the Baroque recorder that Bruce Haynes (maker of baroque oboes from California) has been showing students how to make new blocks for their recorders to improve their tone. As for the music, the old treatises have been studied anew and applied in performance, earlier recordings have been disowned and the music re-recorded in the light of research, and the mannered style of the French baroque has been convincingly revived.

Brüggen has also encouraged the work of *avant-garde* composers and performed their works in his recitals everywhere: *Muziek voor Altblokfluit* by Rob du Bois, L. Andriessen's *Sweet* for recorder, Berio's *Gesti* and Makoto Shinohara's *Fragmente*. In these solo works the simple design of the recorder lends itself particularly well to the interpretation of the *avant-garde* vocabulary with its fluttertongueing, *vibrato,* use of special fingerings, 'chords', *glissandi* and other effects, without the intervention of key mechanism.

While Brüggen has concentrated on the baroque and the *avant garde* Kees Otten replaced his *Muziekkring Obrecht* with *Syntagma Musicum,* a highly professional group of singers and players who perform sixteenth-century and earlier music with an instrumentarium of viols, krummhorns, shawms, portative organ, etc, as well as recorders. Everything that Kees Otten does in music has an air of spontaneity and quiet enjoyment giving the impression that the earliest music was composed only yesterday.

Brüggen's style is individual and he would seem to break all the old rules and get away with it! No standing or sitting upright in order to breathe well—he sits with legs crossed, almost crouching over his recorder, the instrument almost upright. He will justify this by saying that, as he is tall, he would feel too far away from his harpsichordist or the players in the orchestra if he stood up: the recorder is lowered so that its tone is projected towards the audience and not lost among the rafters. Much criticized is the 'Brüggen bulge', the 'wow, wow' on each note, starting below the note, rising with a slight *crescendo* and falling again, the sound being accompanied by a pushing forward of the instrument—an expressive device used by jazz musicians from Stephane Grappelli downwards, but not normally accepted in straight music. To Brüggen it is a 'mannerism' aiming at flexibility.

Frans Brüggen has attracted a very large number of pupils at the conservatoires at The Hague and Amsterdam, in America and in the course of the many master classes and summer schools where he has taught. Among these are Jeanette van Wingerden who has partnered him in many performances, Hans Linnartz, Walter van Hauwe and Kees Boeke (the other members of Brüggen's *Sourcream* trio), Ricardo Kanji (from Brazil) and Baldrick Deerenburg (who teaches at the conservatoire at Antwerp). These are some of the best pupils, but there are many others and the problem with some is that they tend to copy the mannerisms and miss the fundamental musicianship.

Italy had little to show until after 1968 when a number of 'students' from around Turin attended one of the Anglo-French courses at Weymouth. Sergio Balestracci emerged as their leader and organized similar courses in Italy at Mondovi (1971 and 1972) and Pavia (1973), forming at the same time the *Accademia del Flauto Dolce*. Meanwhile in 1970 *La Società del Flauto Dolce* was founded in Rome and its first publication appeared in 1971. This second recorder society is organized by Giancarlo Rostirolla, and publishes music as well as the journal. Near Palermo in Sicily lives Danilo Dolci, and his son, Amico, has become an outstanding virtuoso of the recorder. Amico Dolci (b. 1957) studied first with Edwin Alton, but from 1970 onwards Ferdinand Conrad and I have visited the Dolcis at Trappeto to teach Amico and his sister Daniela who also plays very well. Amico is studying composition at Palermo with Eliodoro Sollima who has written a very fine Sonata for recorder and piano.

There is some recorder playing in Spain and Portugal, unfortunately much of it using German-fingered instruments. It must not be forgotten that the little pipe whose gay flourish starts off the music of the sardana bands of Barcelona is virtually a sopranino recorder. Czechoslovakia and Jugoslavia both have their folk instruments of whistle type, examples of which are shown on Plate II. It will be seen that the Jugoslavs have a double pipe. Another kind of double pipe which was made in the eighteenth century can be seen in Plate XIV, while a nineteenth-century version is shown on Plate XVII. The Czechoslovakian flute (Plate II) is constructed with the wind-way and lip at the back, like some sixteenth-century recorders. It is a six-holed pipe.

The recorder came to Israel from Germany, but is now established there and used extensively in the schools. As a composer, Zvi Herbert Nagan is cultivating an individual national style.

Inquiries show that the recorder is taught in a number of schools in South Africa—at Johannesburg, Pretoria, Mafeking, Queenstown, Krugersdorf and Greytown; at Virginia in the Orange Free State and at Marandellas in Rhodesia. Students from Trinity College of Music, London, have taken recorders to the heart of the Sudan, Nigeria and other tropical parts, where the plastic instruments can be expected to withstand the climate and the ravages of ants.

My inquiries in India and Pakistan have revealed a depressing situation as far as European music is concerned. From Nagpur: 'since 1956 there are very few who take any interest in European Music' and from Poona: 'since Independence Day the Government has tried year by year to crush Western music, and we who have had Western music all our lives find it very difficult to foster it', and 'I understand that there is only one German lady here, the wife of an Indian, who owns and plays on a recorder in Calcutta'. The owner of a music shop in Madras wrote: 'There are a few amateur groups who fancied this instrument, to whom we have sold about a dozen last year, imported from Germany'.

Further East, in Thailand and Malaya, there are students who have studied the recorder in London, and a correspondent in Hong Kong reported that, although the recorder is virtually unknown in adult circles, it is taught there in both English and Chinese schools, usually as an extra-curricular activity, but sometimes in the music lesson. There are classes for recorders in the Hong Kong Music Festival.

By all reports the pockets of interest in the vast continent of Australia have grown, but it is difficult to maintain sufficient contact to gauge the extent of such increase. Australia has, however an outstanding recorder maker in Fred Morgan, and he is also an excellent player.

New Zealand benefited from the impetus given by Carl Dolmetsch's tour soon after World War II, and there have been many contacts with England. Layton Ring, and John Thomson (who for a number of years edited the *Recorder and Music Magazine*) now live here. Alec Loretto has spent some time in Europe studying recorder making and has now set up his workshop in Auckland.

But before all this activity Ronald and Zillah Castle of Wellington were doing the pioneer work. This brother and sister team have lectured, played, broadcast and taught. Their home is like a museum of early instruments, and their collection includes a fine tenor recorder by Stanesby senior which was given to them by Miss D. B. Heath, a music teacher who had been to one of their demonstrations and whose father had brought it out from England.

In Canada the recorder is used in some schools in Ontario, Quebec, New Brunswick, Newfoundland, and Nova Scotia. In many cases it is used as a 'pre-band' instrument, to teach the elements of finger control and breathing; in others, as an instrument in its own right. The leading exponent of the instrument is Mario Duschenes whose *Method for the Recorder* is published by

BMI Canada Ltd, of Toronto. The Huggett Family from Ottawa (Leslie and Margaret, and their children: Andrew, Jennifer, Ian and Fiona) all play recorders as well as krummhorns, viols, etc, and have brought early music to thousands through their concerts.

There are a few players in the British Caribbean Federation, but I have not heard of any in South America, apart from Rolf Alexander and his wife Noelle de Mosa (formerly principal dancers in the Ballets Jooss) who went to Santiago, Chile, where they formed (1954) a group to play music for recorders, viol and lute.

For some time now Japan has been making plastic recorders for the European and American markets. Early examples were poor, most of them with German fingering, until the appearance of the Aulos series. Since then they have produced an admirable copy of the Coolsma treble in plastic. The first number of a magazine *Recorder* (in Japanese) came out in 1972, and there is a fairly comprehensive method of 177 pages with 28-page recorder part. The music includes arrangements of Couperin, Bach, Handel and Telemann.

Left to the end of this survey, we come to the United States of America, where there is a flourishing American Recorder Society. This was founded in 1939 by Suzanne Bloch, lutenist daughter of the composer, who had studied with Arnold Dolmetsch. It seems to have been dormant during the latter part of World War II but to have been revived by Dr Erich Katz (1900-1973) of Santa Barbara in 1947. We remember Dr Katz who spent some time in England, before leaving for the U.S.A. He was a pupil of Willibald Gurlitt and took part in the revivals of early music in the 1920s (in which Peter Harlan also played a part), and later became an assistant at the Musicological Institute at Freiburg. It would appear, to judge from the News-Letters (which became *The American Recorder* in 1960) that the course of the Society has been roughly parallel to that of the English Society, publishing some music and forming Chapters, as the American branches are called. The Society's President (1960), LaNoue Davenport, toured Europe in 1960 with the New York Pro Musica, giving concerts and presenting *The Play of Daniel,* in the accompaniment of which recorders took part.

LaNoue Davenport is a sensitive player who gave a fine performance of a Handel sonata at the 1960 *Recorder in Education* Summer School which he visited before returning to U.S.A.

Bernard Krainis, another brilliant player, also grew up through the A.R.S. and the New York Pro Musica before turning soloist. He visited England in 1965. Martha Bixler, a pupil of LaNoue Davenport, is probably best known as a teacher. Kenneth Wollitz, President of A.R.S. 1974 studied with Kees Otten in Amsterdam.

The impression I have is that the American Recorder Society is interested in the instrument as a means of interpreting the early music, also of playing the modern; but not so much as a school instrument. The use of the instrument in schools is as a 'pre-band' instrument rather than as an instrument to be studied for its own sake, but this is changing, and excellent work in the educational field is being done, for example, by Gene Reichenthal and Gerald Burakoff on Long Island.

David Dushkin was one of the pioneers of the recorder in the U.S.A. and contrived a plastic recorder of original design, with a removable wooden fipple. This was very easy and full in tone owing to its wide bore, but the tone was also rather coarse.

Dushkin started making recorders in 1934 and was followed two years later by Koch of Haverhill, New Hampshire. Now Friedrich von Huene of Brookline, Mass. occupies a leading position among makers. Large numbers of recorders are also imported from Germany (East and West) and from England. For music America is largely dependent on Europe; though there is a growing interest among American composers in the recorder, and Alan Hovhaness has composed a Sextet for recorder, string quartet and harpsichord, Op. 164, which he dedicated to Carl Dolmetsch and Joseph Saxby. From among the recorder players, there are compositions and arrangements by Erich Katz, LaNoue Davenport, Elna Sherman, Bernard Krainis and others.

Professor Dayton Miller (1866-1941) of the Case School of Applied Science, Cleveland, Ohio, was interested in everything concerning the flute, and took the recorder within the orbit of this interest. He brought together the largest collection of flutes in the world, together with a library of books on the subject, and these are now housed at the Library of Congress (see Plate XI). He was a vice-president of the (British) Society of Recorder Players, and watched with interest our work in this field. Other collections of recorders are to be found at the Metropolitan Museum of Art, New York, where there is a copy of the Antwerp great bass; and at the Boston Museum of Fine Arts where there are some recorders of sixteenth-century type made in London and finished by Canon Galpin.

Everywhere more attention has been focussed on early music and in particular that of the renaissance. In 1962 John Cousen began to make his Great Consort of recorders: the double bass in F, great bass in C, Basset in F and tenor in C. Since then Moeck, Hopf and others have added some renaissance-type recorders (in the smaller sizes) to their baroque ranges. Groups specializing in mediaeval and renaissance music have sprung up everywhere: David Munrow with his Early Music Consort, Christopher Ball and his Praetorius Consort are only two of many in England, Yves Audard was the recorder player in *Les Menestriers* of Paris. Kees Otten, a pioneer in this field, now leads his *Syntagma Musicum* of Amsterdam. In Warsaw, Professor Piwkowski has made all the krummhorns, regal, etc, for his *Fistulatores et Tubicinatores Varsovieneses* but has to manage with inferior recorders from Germany (DDR) until he has time to make his own copies after Praetorius. The Studio der *Frühen Musik München* was established in 1960 and the New York Pro Musica in 1961. Many of these groups are attached to universities in U.K., U.S.A. and Canada, such as the Landini Consort of York.

After writing about recorder players round the world I must not end without referring in more detail to recorder making today. In the early days of the revival instruments were individually made by craftsmen like Arnold Dolmetsch. In England these followed baroque models: Praetorius provided the pattern in Germany. In England makers had the example of the narrow windway and concentrated, slightly reedy tone of instruments by Stanesby and Bressan: in Germany the wider bore of the renaissance type favoured a more open tone. At first the wood used was generally of a kind known to be good for instrument making, such as ebony, box, cocus or rosewood. Mass production started in Germany and led to the use of less dense hardwoods, maple and pear, and these had to be treated—impregnated with paraffin wax or other filler—to give them the density necessary for use in instrument making. In England the baroque model was well established, while mass-produced instruments from the continent moved in the same direction, making more English-fingered instruments available. The use of plastics was, during World War II, a temporary expedient; but it was found that, if the design and moulding operations were good, plastic instruments could be better than wooden ones of comparable price. So plastic recorders came to stay.

After the war, with the greatly increasing use of the recorder as a school instrument, a great many new makes appeared, both wooden and plastic, some good, but many very bad—in fact useless as musical instruments. There was a similar anxiety in respect of other instruments supplied to schools, so in 1961 the British Standards Institution set up an advisory committee to prepare a series of Standards setting down in black and white what was required of school instruments. 'B.S. 3499 Part 2A, Recorders' was the result, and this was published in 1964. As a standard it may not be perfect and may need some revision now, but if conscientiously applied it could eliminate many unworthy instruments.

Apart from the Schott and Dolmetsch plastic recorders and Schott's 'Wooden' recorders with plastic mouthpieces, most other school recorders come from Germany or Japan. Of these the Japanese *Aulos* is good, but few of the others would pass the test in the school range. When selecting a descant recorder try the following:

(1) Pitch: this should be a′ =440 and should be tested when the instrument is warm after about 10 minutes playing in a room temperature of 68°F (20°C). It will be *a little* below this pitch when cold.

(2) Intonation:

(i) Try G-F sharp and E-F sharp in both octaves. These should be played with the normal fingerings. If the F sharps are too sharp, don't buy.

(ii) Try the two Es. If the upper E is flat (as on many 'school' recorders from Germany), reject.

(iii) Try B to C sharp and C sharp to D, playing C sharp in the normal way with the first and second fingers of the left hand, and don't accept a C sharp that is too flat. If you are in doubt, try the fifth from F sharp to C sharp.

There are many more possible tests, but the above will quickly eliminate useless instruments.

162

The following are the leading makers of mass-produced recorders in Germany:

In the Federal Republic: Schreiber (Nauheim Kr. Gr. Gerau), Moeck (Celle), Conrad Mollenhauer (Fulda) and Hopf (Wehen bei Wiesbaden).

In the Democratic Republic: Herwig and Adler (both Markneu-kirchen).

Of great importance is the material from which a recorder is made. The best instruments are made from woods which are really hard, such as rosewood, tulip wood, cocus and ebony; but with these the tools have to be constantly re-sharpened. This means that such instruments cannot be mass produced, but demand the highest skill of the craftsman. Box, which used to be the instrument maker's favourite wood, is now rare in a suitable quality. To produce good tone the wood must be close-grained and non-porous; it must also be well seasoned.·

The recorder does not stand still, and makers will continue to try to improve and perfect it. There is the greatest room for improvement in the bass, to strengthen its tone and make it more reliable. Dolmetsch and others have managed to extend the octave and a sixth compass of the instrument to the same two octaves and a note range as the treble, but the danger is that in striving to extend the scope of the instrument in this way, something is lost in its depth and sonority.

The 'improvements' and modifications made by Carl Dolmetsch are: (1) The tone projector. A piece of wood or plastic shaped like the top of a wheel-barrow, which is clipped in front of the opening and lip of the recorder to project the tone forward. This has a double effect, as it also flattens the pitch of the note, making the player blow harder (and louder) to keep in tune. (2) The echo key. Bainbridge's little flageolet (Plate XVII, No. 2) had a key which sharpened the whole instrument by opening a small hole near the mouthpiece. Dolmetsch has placed such a hole at the back of the head joint, and provided it with a key worked by the player's chin! With this device you can play a note firmly with the normal breath and the hole closed: open the hole and blow very gently, and you can play the same note softly. (3) The key for top F sharp on the treble (or C sharp, if fitted to the descant). We have long known that this note can be produced by stopping the end of the recorder while fingering top G. This can also be effected by a simple key mechanism, or by stopping the end of the recorder permanently (remembering to provide a small hole for 'drainage' purposes) and boring a new 'end' to the instrument at the side. This new hole can then be covered by an open-standing key.

These modifications do not spoil the instrument, as it is still basically the same and can be used without touching any of them; but they do help the player when balanced against modern strings in modern music.

In 1971 Daniel Waitzman put forward, under the aegis of the American Recorder Society, a plan to promote the development of a modernized recorder—a bell-keyed instrument that would be the equivalent of the Boehm flute.

M. Louis Stien was awarded a silver medal in the international Salon of Inventors at the Brussels exhibition of 1958, for his *flûte d'amour*. M. Stien was principal oboeist at the Paris Opera until his recent retirement; but the story of his *flûte d'amour* started in 1926, when he revived the *flûte à bec,* first in Paris and then at Cannes, under the direction of Phillipe Gaubert, the celebrated flautist and conductor. This flûte d'amour is a *flûte à bec* of the proportions of a tenor recorder, but fitted with the key mechanism of a modern oboe, enabling the oboeist, as in the time of Purcell or Bach, to play all the recorder as well as the oboe parts. It also opened up possibilities for playing the more chromatic romantic music of a Chopin or a Grieg, as well as arrangements of Scarlatti, Bach and Handel, or of Debussy, Fauré or Ravel. M. Stien showed me three models of his *flûte d'amour,* which he had himself made: (1) *avec plateaux bombés* (keys with rounded tops) for oboeists, (2) *avec plateaux incurvés* (concave) for flautists; and (3) *avec anneaux et réglage simplifié* (with ring-keys and a simplified arrangement) for amateurs. M. Stien played some pieces from the repertoire which he has created for his instrument; and I felt that here was a thoroughly professional instrument, but not a recorder.

Key mechanism was added, in the nineteenth century, to the French flageolet, when it was being used in the quadrille bands. Semitone keys were also applied to the recorder—an example can be seen in Brussels. The recorder, which lends itself to cross-fingered semitones, does not need semitone keys; so M. Stien was right to invent an entirely new kind of fipple-flute.

As to the tone of modern recorders, a slight edge or reediness is desirable in a solo instrument; but school instruments, for class use, should be more gentle and flute-like. Few of the modern recorders I have tried come up to the Bressan treble for tone quality and ease of tone production, with its full and firm low notes. In my experience the recorders of Fred Morgan, von Huene and Coolsma come nearest to this ideal. Most modern recorders are like Mattheson's instruments (see page 72) on account of their wide wind-ways. The narrow channel of the old Bressan provides something to blow against—support for the breath column—so that the technique of playing it is closer to the technique of the flute, oboe and clarinet. This is the direction in which makers of soloist's instruments should aim, leaving the school instruments as they are.

In the making of school recorders we could learn much from the sixteenth-century recorders with the wider bore and fuller low notes; but then teachers and arrangers of school music would have to be content with the smaller, octave and a sixth, compass of such instruments.

The revival of the recorder which we are witnessing is founded on a love of the music of Purcell, Bach and Handel—and Telemann— and the need for a simple means of musical expression, available for amateurs. By these standards it will grow and flourish. The popularity of the seventeenth and eighteenth centuries was a thing of fashion, and doomed to be superseded by the next fashion—the German flute.

So long as composers try to understand the instrument for which they are writing, recorder players will co-operate by trying to understand and interpret their music. If they neglect this simple courtesy, their music will soon be as dead as the dodo.

APPENDIX

A NOTE FOR COMPOSERS

When writing for the recorders, try and have a clear idea of what players you are addressing. Is your music to be played in school, by amateurs, or is it a professional concert piece, or work for a chamber recital? The use for which your music is designed should influence your choice of instruments. Children of eight don't play tenors and basses: amateur groups prefer the more mellow tones of trebles and tenors. Most amateurs who take their recorders at all seriously play 'the lot'—descant, treble, tenor and bass, and, possibly, the sopranino. There may not be more than a score of great basses in England, so it is not yet wise to write independent parts for them—let them double the bass line, occasionally playing an octave lower, where their extra depth is valuable.

Fig. 62

The preceding table gives the range of the normal instruments. They can play in any key, but some keys are easier and more effective than others.

Owing to the cross-fingerings of the recorder, diatonic scales are more effective (and easier) than chromatic runs. But why not try and play the instrument a little yourself? This personal contact with the instrument has undoubtedly contributed to the success of such composers as Britten, Walter Leigh, Baines and others in this medium. Lack of it has not helped some others who shall be nameless!

Points to observe when writing for recorders include: (1) pitch— Praetorius noticed that recorders seem to be an octave lower than they really are—this is mainly due to the strength of the fundamental in relation to the upper partials in the make-up of recorder tone. So when writing for recorders and strings, treat the former as a four-foot choir sounding an octave higher, not in unison with the strings where they would be drowned. (2) Watch for the resultants tones, particularly when writing thirds high up. These resultants are very strong with the pure tone of recorders, and can sometimes spoil the effect of a passage which might be quite effective on other instruments. (3) School tenors generally have a key for the low C, which precludes low C sharp. Many amateurs use similar instruments, so that it would be wise to avoid that note except possibly in music intended for professionals who may be expected to have the necessary double holes. (4) The same applies in the case of low F sharp on bass recorders and low C sharp on great basses — you are unlikely to hear such notes. (5) If in doubt as to which trills are difficult and which impossible, consult one of the more advanced methods.

BIBLIOGRAPHY

PERIODICALS

THE AMERICAN RECORDER SOCIETY NEWS LETTER: Edited 1950—March 1953 by Bernard Krainis, June 1953—1959 by LaNoue Davenport.

THE AMERICAN RECORDER: A quarterly publication of the American Recorder Society, Winter 1960—, edited by Martha Bixler, Ralph Taylor, Donna Hill, Elloyd Hanson, John Koch and Daniel Shapiro.

IL FLAUTO DOLCE: Journal of the Società Italiana del Flauto Dolce, edited by Giancarlo Rostirolla, Rome, 1971—.

DER BLOCKFLÖTEN-SPIEGEL: Edited by F. J. Giesbert, Bonn and published by Hermann Moeck, Celle, Hannover, 1931-34.

THE CONSORT: Journal of the Dolmetsch Foundation, 1930— Edited by Robert Donington (1-4), Dorothy Swainson (5-16), Richard Noble (17-28) and Shelagh Godwin (29—).

EARLY MUSIC: Edited by J. M. Thomson, 1973—.

THE GALPIN SOCIETY JOURNAL, 1948—. In addition to the main articles, items relating to the recorder have often appeared in the correspondence columns, in particular from No. X (1957) onwards.

THE PROCEEDINGS OF THE MUSICAL ASSOCIATION: 1874-1944 (August).

THE PROCEEDINGS OF THE ROYAL MUSICAL ASSOCIATION: 1944—.

THE RECORDER NEWS: The journal of the Society of Recorder Players, 1937—.
Nos. 1-4 (1937-41) edited by Carl Dolmetsch and Edgar Hunt.
No. 5 (-1947) edited by Edgar Hunt.
News-Letters from February 1948—September 1949 (1-5) edited by C. Kenworthy.
The Recorder News, New Series, No. 1, February 1950, edited by C. Kenworthy.

Magazine of the Society of Recorder Players, Junior Section, edited by Freda Dinn, December 1949–May 1955.

THE RECORDER AND MUSIC MAGAZINE: incorporating *The Recorder News:* in May 1963 this quarterly, edited by C. Kenworthy, continued as the Journal of the S.R.P. In August 1964 Ronald Corcoran took over as editor. Since then the editors have been successively J. M. Thomson (July 1966), Ronald Corcoran (August 1967), and J. M. Thomson (June 1971), Edgar Hunt (December 1974).

THE SUSSEX RECORDER NEWS: The journal of the Sussex Recorder Players, No. 1-7 (Christmas 1950–Midwinter 1954) edited by Stanley Godman.

DIE ZEITSCHRIFT FÜR HAUSMUSIK: 1934-49, Journal of the Arbeitskreis für Hausmusik. Bärenreiter-Verlag, Kassel.

SONORUM SPECULUM: Published quarterly by the Donemus Foundation to promote Dutch music. In Summer 1967 Michael Vetter wrote on *New Recorder Music from Holland* and in Spring 1970 Wouter Paap wrote on *Frans Brüggen and the Recorder.*

ARTICLES and LECTURES

Dr JOSEPH COX BRIDGE: *The Chester Recorders,* in the Proceedings of the Musical Association, February 12, 1901.

EMIL BRAUER: *Blockflöten,* in Der Kreis (Arbeits- und Mitteilungsblatt für Singkreis), May 1928.

ADAM CARSE: *Fingering the Recorder,* in The Music Review No. 2.

THURSTON DART: *Bach's 'Flauti d'Echo'* in Music and Letters 41/4, October 1960.

CARL DOLMETSCH: *The Dolmetsch Tradition,* in Music Parade, Vol. 1, No. 4 (n.d., ? 1947).

CARL DOLMETSCH: *Early Musical Instruments,* a lecture given on Nov. 8, 1947 to the Institute of Musical Instrument Technology.

CARL DOLMETSCH: *The Recorder, its history, design and resources discussed,* in Woodwind Book 1957-8, edited by Brian

Manton-Myall. Boosey & Hawkes, 1957.

CARL DOLMETSCH: *The Recorder or English Flute*, in Music and Letters, 1941.

H. MACAULAY FITZGIBBON: *Of Flutes and Soft Recorders* in The Musical Quarterly, April 1934.

KERL GÖRISCHK: *Die Blockflöte in der Schulmusik*, in Collegium Musicum (Blatter zur Pflege der Haus- und Kammermusik) 1932/ii.

W. H. GRATTAN FLOOD: *Entries relating to Music in the English Patent Rolls of the Fifteenth Century*, from The Musical Antiquary, July 1913.

EDGAR HUNT: The articles on 'Recorder' in Grove's Dictionary and in Percy Scholes's Oxford Companion to Music.

EDGAR HUNT: *The Recorder or English Flute*, in The Amateur Musician, No. 3, 1935.

ARNDT von LÜPKE: *Untersuchung an Blockflöten* in *Akustische Zeitschrift* 5th year, 1940.

CHARLES STUART: *'Dolmetscherie' Today,* in The Musical Times, July 1951.

CHRISTOPHER WELCH: *Hamlet and the Recorder,* in The Proceedings of the Musical Association, 1902.

CHRISTOPHER WELCH: *Literature relating to the Recorder,* in The Proceedings of the Musical Association, 1898.

WALDEMAR WOEHL: *Handhabung und Verwendung der Blockflöte*, in Die Musikantengilde (Blatter der Werbereitung für Jugend und Volk) July 1928.

BOOKS and PAMPHLETS

ANTHONY BAINES: Catalogue of Musical Instruments at the Victoria and Albert Museum, Vol. II Non-Keyboard Instruments, Her Majesty's Stationery Office, London, 1968.

ANTHONY BAINES (Editor): *Musical Instruments through the ages*, Penguin Books, London, 1961.

ANTHONY BAINES: *Woodwind Instruments and their History*, Faber, London, 1957.

BRUNO BARTOLOZZI: *New Sounds for Woodwind,* translated by Reginald Smith Brindle, Oxford University Press, London, 1967.

A. BERNER, J. H. van der MEER & G. THIBAULT: *Preservation and Restoration of Musical Instruments,* Evelyn, Adams and Mackay, London, 1967.

NICHOLAS BESSARABOFF: *Ancient European Musical Instruments,* with a Preface by E. J. Hipkins and a Foreword by Canon Francis Galpin, Harvard University Press for the Museum of Fine Arts, Boston, 1941.

Dr ALEXANDER BUCHNER: *Musical Instruments through the Ages,* translated by Iris Urwin, Spring Books, London, n.d.

GERALD BURAKOFF: *The Recorder in the Classroom,* Hargail, New York, 1971.

Dr CHARLES BURNEY: *A General History of Music,* 4 vols. T. Becket, J. Robson and G. Robinson, London, 1776.

Dr CHARLES BURNEY: *The Present State of Music in Germany, The Netherlands and United Provinces,* 2 vols, T. Becket, J. Robson and G. Robinson, London, 1773.

ADAM CARSE: *Catalogue of the Adam Carse collection of old Musical Wind Instruments.* L. C. C. Horniman Museum, London, 1951. (Also earlier lists of the same collection).

ADAM CARSE: *Musical Wind Instruments,* Methuen, London, 1939.

F. B. CHAPMAN: *Flute Technique,* Oxford University Press London, 19—.

CARL CLAUDIUS' *Samling of Gamle Musikinstrumenter.* Levin & Munksgaards Forlag, Copenhagen, 1931.

CSAKAN-SCHULE: B. Schott's Söhne, Mainz, n.d. (?1830)

ULRICH DAUBENEY: *Orchestral Wind Instruments,* W. Reeves, London, 1920.

DIETZ DEGEN: *Zur Geschichte der Blockflöte in den germanischen Ländern,* Bärenreiter-Verlag, Kassel, n.d.

FREDA DINN: *The Recorder in School,* Schott, London, 1965.

ARNOLD DOLMETSCH: *The Interpretation of the Music of the Seventeenth and Eighteenth Centuries,* Novello, London, 1915.

CARL DOLMETSCH: *Music and Craftsmanship* in *Fifteen Craftsmen on their Crafts,* edited by John Farleigh, Sylvan Press, London, 1945.

ROBERT DONINGTON: *The Work and Ideas of Arnold Dolmetsch,* The Dolmetsch Foundation, Haslemere, 1932.

ROBERT DONINGTON: *The Instruments of Music,* Methuen, London, 1949.

GEORGES DUHAMEL: *Histoire et Richesses de la Flûte,* Librarie Gründ, Paris, 1953.

CARL ENGEL: *Musical Instruments,* Chapman and Hall, London, 1875.

CARL ENGEL: *Descriptive Catalogue of the Musical Instruments in the South Kensington Museum,* 2nd Edition, Eyre and Spottiswoode, London, 1874.

JOHN EVELYN: *Diary,* edited by William Bray, Dent, London, 1907.

J. FINN: *The Recorder, Flute, Fife and Piccolo* in *English Music* (Lectures given at the Music Loan Exhibition, Fishmongers' Hall. 1904), Walter Scott Co., London, 1911.

H. MACAULAY FITZGIBBON: *The Story of the Flute,* W. Reeves, London, 1928.

JEAN-PIERRE FREILLON-PONCEIN: *La véritable manière d'apprendre à jouer en perfection du Hautbois, de la Flûte et du Flageolet,* Jacques Collombat, Paris, 1700: facsimile, Minkoff Reprints, Geneva, 1971.

Canon FRANCIS W. GALPIN: *Old English Instruments of Music,* Methuen, London, 1910.

Canon FRANCIS W. GALPIN: *A textbook of European Musical Instruments,* Williams and Norgate, London, 1937.

THE GALPIN SOCIETY: *British Musical Instruments*—Exhibition Catalogue, London, 1951.

SYLVESTRO GANASSI: *Opera initulata Fontegara,* Venice, 1535. Edited by Dr. Hildemarie Peter, English translation (1959) by Dorothy Swainson from the German edition (1956). Robert Lienau, Berlin Lichterfelde.

KARL GEIRINGER: *Musical Instruments,* translated by Bernard Miall and edited by W. F. H. Blandford, Allen and Unwin, London, 1943.

ANGUL HAMMERICH: *Das Musikhistorische Museum zu Kopenhagen,* G. E. C. Gad, Kopenhagen, 1911.

Sir JOHN HAWKINS: *A General History of the Science and Practice of Music,* 5 vols., T. Payne, London, 1776.

A. J. HIPKINS: *Guide to the Loan Collection of Musical Instruments at the International Inventions Exhibition,* Clowes, London, 1885.

A. J. HIPKINS & WILLIAM GIBB: *Musical Instruments, Historic, Rare and Unique,* Adam & Charles Black, Edinburgh, 1888.

HOTTETERRE le Romain: *L'Art de Préluder,* edited by M. Sanvoisin, Zurfluh, Paris, 1966.

Le Sieur HOTTETERRE-LE-ROMAIN: *Principes de la Flûte Traversière ou Flûte d'Allemagne, de la Flûte à Bec, ou Flûte Douce, et du Hautbois,* Estienne Roger, Amsterdam, 1707: facsimile with German translation by Hans Joachim Hellwig, Bärenreiter-Verlag, Kassel, 1941: English translation with introduction by David Lasocki, Barry & Rockliff, London, 1968; English translation by P. M. Douglas, Dover, New York, 1968.

EDGAR HUNT: *The Recorder—a handbook of useful information,* Schott, London, 1957.

PHILIBERT JAMBE DE FER, *Epitome Musical, Paris,* 1556. Facsimile with introduction by François Lesure, Société de Musique d'Autrefois, Neuilly-sur-Seine, 1963.

JEAN JENKINS: *Musical Instruments,* Horniman Museum, London 1958.

GEORG KINSKY: *A History of Music in Pictures,* Dent, London, 1930.

HERBERT KÖLBEL: *Von der Flöte,* Staufen-Verlag, Köln & Krefeld, 1951.

HENRY CART DE LAFONTAINE: *The King's Musick,* 1460-1700, Novello, London, 1909.

LYNDESAY LANGWILL: *An Index of Musical Wind-Instrument Makers,* published by the author, Edinburgh 1960. The fourth edition (1974) includes a section devoted to makers' marks.

LYNDESAY LANGWILL: *Recorder Makers*—duplicated list, June 1952.

HANS-MARTIN LINDE: *Handbuch des Blockflötenspiels,* B. Schott's Söhne, Mainz, 1962: English translation by J. C. Haden, 1974.

HANS-MARTIN LINDE: *Kleine Anleitung zum Verzieren alter Musik,* B. Schott's Söhne, Mainz, 1958.

VICTOR CHARLES MAHILLON: *Catalogue Descriptif et Analytique du Musée Instrumental du Conservatoire Royal de Musique de Bruxelles*—Deuxième volume—Deuxième Edition, Ad. Haste, Gand, 1909.

JOSEPH FRIEDRICH BERNHARD CASPAR MAJER: *Museum Musicum,* facsimile edited by Heinz Becker, Bärenreiter-Verlag, Kassel & Basel, 1954.

JOHN MANIFOLD: *The Amorous Flute,* Workers' Music Association, London, 1948.

JOHN MANIFOLD: *The Music in English Drama,* Rockliff, London, 1956.

N. MAUGER: *Les Hotteterres—Nouvelles recherches,* Fischbacher, Paris, 1912.

MARIN MERSENNE: *Harmonie universelle, contenant la theorie et la practique de la musique,* Paris, 1736.

Dr ERNST HERMANN MEYER: *Die Mehrstimmige Spielmusik in des 17 Jahrhunderts in Nord- und Mitteleuropa,* Bärenreiter Verlag, Kassel, 1934.

DAYTON C. MILLER: *List of Instrument Makers* represented by specimens in the Dayton C. Miller Collection of Flutes, duplicated, Cleveland, Ohio, 1935.

DAYTON C. MILLER: *Catalogue of Books and Literary Material relating to the Flute,* privately printed, Cleveland, Ohio, 1935.

From the MODERN MUSIC MASTER: *Instructions and tunes for the Treble Recorder,* facsimile from the original of 1731, with note by Edgar Hunt, Schott, London, 1957.

C.D.NEDERVEEN: *Acoustical aspects of Woodwind Instruments,* Frits Knuf, Amsterdam, 1969.

GEORG NUENER: *Musikinstrumenten aus Bach'scher Zeit,* Catalogue of an exhibition at Schaffhausen, 1957.

Bibliography

ROGER NORTH: *Autobiography,* edited by Dr Jessopp, David Nutt, London, 1889.

SAMUEL PEPYS: *Diary,* edited by Richard Lord Braybroke, Dent, London, 1924.

Dr HILDEMARIE PETER: *The Recorder, its traditions and its tasks,* English translation by Stanley Godman, Robert Lienau, Berlin Lichterfelde, 1958.

Dr HILDEMARIE PETER: *Die Blockflöte und ihre Spielweise in Vergangenheit und Gegenwart,* Robert Lienau, Berlin Lichterfelde, 1953.

MICHAEL PRAETORIUS: *De Organographia—Syntagma Musicum II,* Wolfenbüttel, 1619, facsimile edited by Willibald Gurlitt, Bärenreiter-Verlag, Kassel, 1929.

JOHANN JOACHIM QUANTZ: *Versuch einer Anweisung die Flûte traversière zu spielen,* Breslau, 1789, facsimile edited by Hans-Peter Schmitz, Bärenreiter-Verlag, Kassel, 1953.

C. VAN RAALTE: *Catalogue of the sale* of the Collection of Musical Instruments at Brownsea Castle, with note by Canon Galpin, 1927.

Dr E. G. RICHARDSON: *Wind Instruments from Musical and Scientific Aspects.* Royal Society of Arts, Cantor Lectures, London, 1929.

F. F. RIGBY: *Playing the Recorders,* Faber, London, 1958.

TREVOR ROBINSON: *The Amateur Wind Instrument Maker,* The University of Massachusetts Press, 1973.

R. S. ROCKSTRO: *A Treatise on . . . the Flute,* Rudall, Carte, London, 1928.

EVELYN ROTHWELL: *Oboe Technique,* Oxford University Press, London, 1953.

A. ROWLAND-JONES: *Recorder Technique,* Oxford University Press, London, 1959.

CURT SACHS: *The History of Musical Instruments,* Norton, New York, 1940.

CURT SACHS: *Real-Lexikon der Musikinstrumente,* Julius Bard, Berlin, 1913.

P. SAMBAMOORTHY: *The Flute,* Indian Music Publishing House, Madras, 1927.

MAX SAUERLANDL: *Die Musik in fünf Jahrhunderten der Europäischen Malerei (Musical Instruments in Pictures),* K. R. Langeweische, Königstein im Taunus, William Reeves, London, 1922.

GUSTAV SCHECK: *Die Längsflöte,* from Der Weg zu den Holz-blasininstrumenten (Vol. IV of Hohe Schule der Musik edited Dr Joseph Müller-Blattau) Akademische Verlagsgessellschaft Athanaion mbH, Potsdam, 1935.

GUSTAV SCHECK: *Die Flöte und ihre Musik,* B. Schotts Söhne, Mainz, 1975.

JULIUS SCHLOSSER: *Kleiner Führer durch die Sammlung alter Musikinstrumente,* Verlag der Kunsthistorischen Sammlungen, Wien, 1933.

JULIUS SCHLOSSER: *Unsere Musikinstrumente,* Kunstverlag Anton Schroll, Wien, 1922.

RUDOLPH SCHOCH: *Blockflötenstunden—Eine Wegleitung für den Anfänger-Gruppenunterricht,* Hug, Zurich, 1947.

HANS PETER SCHMITZ: *Querflöte und Querflötenspiel in Deutschland während des Barockzeitalters,* Bärenreiter-Verlag, Kassel, 1952.

F. SMEKENS: *Stad Antwerpen, Ouheid kundige Musea Vleeshuis Catalogus V Muziekinstrumenten,* Govaerts, Deurne-Antwerpen, n.d.

PHILIP SPITTA: *John Sebastian Bach, his work and influence on the music of Germany* 1685-1750, 3 vols. Novello, London, 1885.

C. S. TERRY: *Bach's Orchestra,* Oxford University Press, London, 1932.

G. THIBAULT (Mme. de Chambure), JEAN JENKINS, J. BRANRICCI: *Eighteenth-Century Musical Instruments: France and Britain (Les instruments de musique au XVIIIe siecle: France et Grande Bretagne)* Victoria and Albert Museum, London,1973.

ERNEST THOINAN: *Les Hotteterres et les Chédevilles,* Edmond Sagot, Paris, 1894.

PIERRE TRICHET: *Traité des Instruments de Musique,* edited by François Lesure, Societe de Musique d'Autrefois, Neuilly-sur-Seine, 1957.

JOHN THOMSON: *Recorder Profiles:* Schott, London, 1972.

JOHN THOMSON: *Your Book of the Recorder,* Faber, London, 1968.

ERICH VALENTIN: *George Philipp Telemann—Eine Biographie,* Fritz Seifert, Hameln, 1947.

MICHAEL VETTER: *Il Flauto Dolce ed Acerbo,* Moeck, Celle, 1969.

SEBASTIAN VIRDUNG: *Musica Getutscht,* Basel 1511, facsimile edited by Leo Schrade, Bärenreiter-Verlag, Kassel, 1931.

LESLIE WARD: *The Dolmetsch Workshops,* Arnold Dolmetsch Ltd, Haslemere, 1949.

JOH. CHRISTOPH WEIGEL: *Musicalisches Theatrum* (c. 1720): facsimile, Bärenreiter-Verlag, Kassel, 1961.

CHRISTOPHER WELCH: *Six Lectures on the Recorder and other Flutes in relation to Literature,* Oxford University Press, 1911.

CHRISTOPHER WELCH: *Lectures on the Recorder,* reprint of the first half of the above which deals with the recorder, with an introduction by Edgar Hunt, Oxford University Press, London, 1961.

OTHMAR WESSELEY: *Die Musikinstrumenten Sammlung des Oberösterreichischen Landesmuseums,* Linz.

LINDE HÖFFER VON WINTERFELD: *Die Solo Blockflöte,* Mitteldeutscher Verlag GmbH, Halle.

LINDE HÖFFER VON WINTERFELD & HARALD KUNZ: *Handbuch der Blockflöten-Literatur,* Bote & Bock, Berlin & Wiesbaden, 1959.

PAUL DE WIT: *Perlen aus der Instrumenten-Sammlung,* Leipzig, 1892.

INDEX

184